Karate:
Pin'an Katas in Depth

Keiji Tomiyama

EMPIRE Books
P.O. Box 491788, Los Angeles, CA 90049

First published in 2004 by SK Enterprises
Published in 2006 by Empire Books. United States of America

06 05 04 03 02 01 00 99 98 97 1 3 5 7 9 10 8 6 4 2
Printed in the United States of America.

Empire Books
P.O. Box 491788
Los Angeles, CA 90049

Library of Congress: 2006009382
ISBN-10: 1-933901-02-0
ISBN-13: 978-1-933901-02-2

Library of Congress Cataloging-in-Publication Data

Tomiyama, Keiji.
  Karate : Pinan katas in depth / by Keiji Tomiyama.
      p. cm.
  Includes index.
  ISBN 1-933901-02-0 (pbk. : alk. paper)
  1. Karate--Japan. 1. Title.
  GV1114.3.T657 2006
  796.815'30952--dc22

2006009382

Shihan Tomiyama is partnered in these photographs by Garry Pettit, 5th Dan Shito-ryu
Karate-do Kofukan

Editing by S. Tomiyama
Photography by Mount Photography, Newark, Notts.
Design and typesetting by Ferdinand Page Design, Surrey

Mrs. Yoko Tadda
650 Western Hills Dr. SE
Rio Rancho, NM 87124

D i s c l a i m e r

Acknowledgements

I would like to thank my wife Sally for editing the text and organizing everything for this book. Without her help, this book could not have been produced.

I would also like to thank Garry Pettit for helping as my partner in the photographs.

About the author

Keiji Tomiyama began training in Tani-ha Shito-ryu while studying at Doshisha University in the sixties, having first learnt boxing at high school followed by Goju-ryu karate on entry to university. He was a successful competitor for the university Karate Club and the West Japan University Students' team.

Sent to Europe by Tani-ha Shito-ryu founder Master Chojiro Tani after graduating, he taught first in Paris, then Brussels. In the late seventies he made England his base, where he has remained except for short spells in Japan dealing with family matters. During those occasions he was able to study with Master H. Fujimoto and other masters who were direct students of Master Kenwa Mabuni.

As head of the Shito-ryu Karate-do Kofukan International organization Keiji Tomiyama's aim is to continue his pursuit of excellence and to pass on knowledge gained through this endeavour both to the association's members and to other karate-ka who value sound principle and good technique. With this goal in mind, as well as producing instructional aids, he directs regular seminars around the world.

Also by Keiji Tomiyama

'FUNDAMENTALS OF KARATE-DO
Essential elements for development through karate training at all levels'

Contents

Part Four

Part Five

Introduction

The five Pin'an Katas are the most widely practised Karate Katas of all. Out of the four major Karate styles three of them, namely Shotokan, Wado-ryu and Shito-ryu, practise Pin'an Katas as part of their basic Katas. Kyokushinkai and Okinawan Shorin-ryu schools practise them as well.

What are Pin'an Katas?

It is said that Pin'an Katas were created by Master Ankoh Itosu (1832 – 1915) when he and his senior students started to teach Karate officially at schools in Okinawa in 1901. Before then, the basic Kata of Shuri-te which students were taught first were Naihanchin (Naifanchi). Because Naihanchin Kata is quite difficult to perform properly, students needed to spend two to three years to learn it. Moreover, as Naihanchin Kata has rather a plain and sombre appearance without any spectacular movement, many students got bored and dropped out, although this formed a part of the process to select keen and loyal students. To avoid this kind of situation with school pupils, Master Itosu created these Pin'an Katas, making them easier to learn with a bigger variety of techniques.

As you will see, there are five Pin'an Katas – Shodan (first step), Nidan (second step), Sandan (third step), Yondan (fourth step) and Godan (fifth step). The first Kata, Shodan, is rather complicated and difficult as the first thing to learn for beginners. Master Itosu must have realised this, so he made the second Kata, Nidan, much simpler and easier. Because of this fact, it is the general practise to teach beginners Nidan first before Shodan. Master Gichin Funakoshi, founder of the Shotokan style of Karate, actually swapped the positions of these Katas and renamed them. So, now Nidan is Shodan (Heian Shodan) and Shodan is Nidan (Heian Nidan). But, other schools did not take this course as they thought keeping the original names was quite important.

Master Funakoshi was the first person to introduce Karate to the mainland of Japan and he tried to rename Katas in the Japanese language rather than keeping the original Okinawan name. Pin'an and Heian are exactly the same word with, of course, the same meaning. The only difference is pronunciation. Pin'an is the original Okinawan/Chinese pronunciation, whereas Heian is Japanese. It means 'peace'. The Japan Karate Federation have now also decided to call their standardised version Heian.

Some critics said that Pin'an Katas were too complicated and too long for beginners. They said that, instead of five, two would have been enough. Maybe they have a point. But, the fact is that Master Itosu created five Pin'an Katas and taught them in schools and that Pin'an katas became the most popular Karate Katas in the world.

Master Itosu created Pin'an Katas using Bassai (Passai) and Kosokun (Kusanku) Katas as the raw material or source. So many movements are similar to these Katas. However, Pin'an Katas are the first Karate Katas made in Okinawa by Okinawans. All previous Karate Katas are 'Okinawanised' but of Chinese origin. Some people point this out and say that Pin'an Katas are the sole pure Shuri-te katas and that one can learn Shuri-te just by practising Pin'an Katas. I can agree with this argument to a certain degree because, despite the fact that they were made for beginners, Pin'an Katas are not low-level Katas. The most popular traditional Shuri-te Kata is Bassai (Passai) and probably the second most popular one is Kosokun (Kusanku). I would say, if someone learnt these two Katas well together with the basic Naihanchin Kata, he or she has achieved a quite good level in Shuri-te. As Pin'an Katas are somewhat a re-arrangement of the first two katas, I can confidently say that, if someone has learnt Pin'an Katas well, he or she has achieved a quite good level of Shuri-te. And anyone who has learnt Pin'an Katas well will have no difficulty in progressing to these two and other traditional Shuri-te Katas.

Variations

Most Karate teachers and founders of various schools of Shuri-te were students of Master Itosu and they learnt Pin'an Katas from him directly but, strangely, there are many variations among them. So, it is almost impossible to define how the original version was. It seems to me that people considered Katas just a tool to practise and had no hesitation to change or vary them according to their personal needs or ideas. But, at least, it can be said that Shito-ryu and Shorin-ryu versions are closer to the original than Shotokan and Wado-ryu versions.

Moreover, even in Shito-ryu groups, there are some variations. The JKF standardised version (Heian) is a Shito-ryu version deriving mainly from the Shito-kai organization. It is different from ours which is, of course, the Tani-ha Shito-ryu version. As there are slight variations within Tani-ha Shito-ryu people as well, the Pin'an Katas I present in this book are, strictly speaking, the standardised versions of the Tani-ha Shito-ryu Karate-do Kofukan organization, of which I am the president and joint chief instructor.

Master Chojiro Tani, founder of Tani-ha Shito-ryu and my teacher, was one of the most senior students of Master Kenwa Mabuni, founder of Shito-ryu and one of the most senior students of Master Ankoh Itosu.

By studying books written by Master Kenwa Mabuni, I know that there are certain differences between what Master Mabuni showed in his book and what I learnt from Master Tani. Actually, as far as I know, none of the Shito-ryu organizations practise Pin'an Katas exactly like Master Mabuni in his book. For example, Master Mabuni used *Ma-hanmi* (side facing) *Nekoashi-dachi* (cat stance) at the beginning of each Kata. No Shito-ryu school currently uses this position and generally *Hanmi* (quarter facing) position is used instead. Also, Master Mabuni used *Re-no-ji-dachi* stance extensively. Again, I have not seen any Shito-ryu organization use this stance in Pin'an

Purposes of Kata practice

Katas. Generally, they use *Moto-dachi* instead, whereas Master Tani more often used *Zenkutsu-dachi*.

All stylistic differences aside, the purposes of training in Kata are, according to Master Mabuni, to learn 1) variety of techniques, 2) control of breathing and 3) smooth transfer of weight. So, first of all, you must learn each of the Kata's component techniques properly. This includes correct stances. Then you must move from one position to the next smoothly and perform the technique without losing balance. While you are performing a Kata, you must control your breathing so that you do not get so out of breath as to hinder your performance and, at the same time, you do not make your breathing pattern too obvious to others (i.e. imaginary opponents).

Master Mabuni also said that you should not think it is enough to just remember the Katas. To get the full benefit, you should practise them every-day for many years, hopefully the rest of your life. By doing so, you will get good health and longevity as well as deeper understanding of techniques.

Principles

For me, the main purpose of training Kata is to learn and practise the technical principles behind each technique. The aim of proper techniques is to produce maximum effect with minimum effort. Of course, it is difficult to achieve this straight away. Inevitably, one makes lots of unnecessary movements and uses lots of excess physical energy to perform each technique and movement at the beginning. As time goes by, one's movement becomes smoother and softer, thus using less energy. As one makes further progress, many movements become so subtle as to become almost invisible to untrained eyes. This involves the greater use of deeper or inner muscles and therefore is called 'internalisation' of techniques. The end result is soft, smooth and coordinated whole-body movements which do not show much trace of force yet are surprisingly powerful.

This is the path of progress and one has to go steadily along this path to progress. It is said that true softness can only be achieved through hardness. You have to train hard and, once you have learnt the movement and order of the Kata, you should try to punch, kick and block as hard, strong and sharp as you can without distorting the technique. In other words, you should try to perform the Kata 'neat' and 'sharp'. Only by training this way will you gradually learn (with the help of your instructors) the proper way to use your energy or force. The more energy you use for the purpose of the technique the better (at least up to a certain level, after which you have to aim to use the least energy and still achieve the purpose of the technique), and the less energy you use which is against or unnecessary for the purpose of the technique the better.

The same can be said about the movement. The movement of the technique should be for the purpose of the technique only. All other movements, i.e. unnecessary or excess movements, will slow down the technique, use unnecessary energy and make unnecessary openings towards the opponent.

So, I summarize the above as follows:`

1 Do not make any unnecessary movement (but make necessary movements).

2 Do not use any unnecessary force (but use necessary force).

3 Use the whole body to perform techniques.

4 Start the next movement from the present position.

Principle 4 above is important for learning the smooth transfer of one's weight and incorporating it with the next technique. A good technique, as I mentioned above, consists of smooth and coordinated whole-body movements. So principle 3 is the most important of these four principles and the other three are principles to help you achieve principle 3. Use of the whole body includes the use of one's whole body weight and principle 4 plays an important role in achieving this.

Another important factor involved in achieving whole-body movements is correct posture. To have correct posture, you have to align your head, neck and trunk in a vertical line. This line is called 'Seichusen' in Japanese, meaning 'correct centre line'. Or, in English, I simply call it 'axis'. By aligning them, you are actually uniting the whole body as one piece : only by doing so will you be able to perform techniques using the whole body.

How to use this book

As you will see, I have divided each Kata into sections and explained the movements of each section in detail then shown its application (Bunkai) with a partner. I hope this will make it easier for you to understand the Kata.

As I mentioned earlier, the Pin'an Katas in the first part of this book which I explain in detail are the standardised versions of Tani-ha Shito-ryu Kofukan.

I have also shown in this book the Japan Karate-do Federation's standardised versions which are called 'Heian'. You will thus see two variations within Shito-ryu. There are several more variations but the differences are not very great from these two versions. As this is only a variation, I have not explained in too much detail and have shown them without any Bunkais.

Kata moves in both the Pin'an Kata sections and Heian Kata sections should be viewed in horizontal rows across each two-page spread. Arrows on kata illustrations indicate the new direction to follow when there is a change of direction.

Practising traditional Karate Katas is a very good method to improve the quality of each technique comprised in these Katas, to widen one's repertoire of techniques and to improve concentration as well as breathing. But, it does not provide the means to improve one's sense of distance, timing, angle and one's ability to feel the opponent's reaction (feedback). 'Bunkai' practices are supposed to serve this purpose. However, to try out certain techniques from Katas at random with a partner does not allow the depth of thought and repetition necessary to refine one's techniques and state of mind in most cases. This is the reason why we created sets like 'Pin'an Kumite' and 'Pin'an Bunkai Kumite', following the example of Master Kenwa Mabuni and his senior students who created 'Hokei Kumite'.

I have covered these sets in three chapters with detailed explanations.

Conclusion

Although it is impossible to learn properly from a book, I have written this book to help students and instructors alike to understand the Pin'an Katas (and Karate in general) better as well as to be an aide-mémoire.

I hope they will appreciate as I do the riches to be found through an in-depth study of Pin'an Katas.

Keiji Tomiyama
January 2004

Pin'an Katas

Pin'an Nidan

Pin'an Nidan

1

Musubi-dachi

2

Rei (bow)

3

Put both hands in front of the solar plexus (right hand on top, both palms facing upwards).

4

Naotte position (The left hand is outside.)
Here, you should announce the name of the Kata.

Sequence 1 Chudan Uchi-otoshi and Chudan Oi-zuki

Look left and open the right heel.

Turn to the left and make left *Nekoashi-dachi* (cat stance) in *Hanmi* position.

At the same time, perform left *Chudan Uchi-otoshi* block. *Uchi-otoshi* (strike down) block must be performed in a circular manner.

5

First, open the left foot, change hands to fists and cross arms.

6

Then open the right foot to make *Heiko-dachi* (parallel stance) while pulling back both arms.

7

Lower the fists in front of the groin to make *Yoi* position

This same beginning is used for all Pin'an Katas.

(front view)

Step forward with the right foot on to right *Zenkutsu-dachi* stance in *Shomen* position. At the same time, perform right *Chudan Oi-zuki.*

Example A Block the opponent's punch with *Uchi-otoshi* block

and counter-attack with *Chudan-zuki*.

into *Nekoashi-dachi* stance and, at the same time, twist and pull the arm as *Uchi-otoshi* movement.

Example B When the opponent grabs your wrist, drop the body

Carry on the circular movement to strike the head of the opponent with *Kentsui* (hammer-fist).

Follow up with *Chudan-zuki*.

Sequence 2 Gedan Harai-uke, Chudan Uchi-otoshi and Chudan Oi-zuki

Step back and across slightly with the right foot so that you can turn into right *Zenkutsu-dachi* stance in *Shomen* position.

At the same time, perform right *Gedan Harai-uke* (sweeping block). The left fist should remain at the side of the body in *Hikite* position.

Shift weight onto the left leg and pull the right foot back slightly to make right *Nekoashi-dachi* stance in *Hanmi* position.

Bunkai

1

Block the opponent's kick with *Harai-uke*.

2

Block the following punch with *Chudan Uchi-otoshi* as you change stance into *Nekoashi-dachi*.

At the same time, perform right *Chudan Uchi-otoshi* block. The left *Hikite* still remains at *Hikite* position.

Step forward with the left foot onto left *Zenkutsu-dachi* stance in *Shomen* position.

At the same time, perform left *Chudan Oi-zuki.*

Follow up with *Chudan-zuki.*

Sequence 3 *Gedan Harai-uke* and *Jodan Age-uke*

Move the left foot towards the left, and make left *Zenkutsu-dachi* stance in *Shomen* position.

At the same time, perform left *Gedan Harai-uke* block. The right fist should remain at *Hikite* position.

(side view)

Step forward with the left foot onto left *Zenkutsu-dachi* stance in *Shomen* position.

At the same time, perform left *Jodan Age-uke* block.

(side view)

Step forward with the right foot on to right *Zenkutsu-dachi* stance in *Shomen* position.

At the same time, perform right *Jodan Age-uke* (upper block).

(side view)

Step forward with the right foot onto right *Zenkutsu-dachi* stance in *Shomen* position.

At the same time, perform right *Jodan Age-uke* block with *Kiai* (shout).

(side view)

Note the body position remains *Shomen* all the way through this sequence, and height remains the same as well.

Example A Slide back a little and block the opponent's kick with *Harai-uke*

Use *Fumikae* step and switch stance.

Follow up straight away with counter punch.

At the same time, block the following *Jodan-zuki* with *Age-uke*.

Example B Block the opponent's *Jodan-zuki* with *Age-uke*, then hold the wrist.

As you twist the wrist outwards, step in and break the elbow with *Age-uke* movement.

Sequence 4 *Gedan Harai-uke* and *Chudan Oi-zuki*

Pivot on the right foot to turn anti-clockwise onto a line at 45 degrees left, moving the left foot to make left *Zenkutsu-dachi* stance in *Shomen* position.

At the same time, perform left *Gedan Harai-uke* block.

Step forward with the right foot onto right *Zenkutsu-dachi* stance in *Shomen* position.

At the same time, perform right *Gedan Harai-uke* block.

Step forward with the left foot onto left *Zenkutsu-dachi* stance in *Shomen* position.

At the same time, perform left *Chudan Oi-zuki*.

At the same time, perform right *Chudan Oi-zuki*.

Move the right foot towards the line at 45 degrees right (so you will change direction through 90 degrees) and make right *Zenkutsu-dachi* stance in *Shomen* position.

Bunkai

1

Block the opponent's punch or kick with *Harai-uke*.

2

Counter-attack with *Chudan-zuki*.

Sequence 5 *Gedan Harai-uke* and *Chudan Oi-zuki*

Move left foot and turn anti-clockwise through 45 degrees to move along a line directly behind the starting position and make left *Zenkutsu-dachi* stance in *Shomen* position.

(side view)

At the same time, perform left *Gedan Harai-uke*. The right fist remains at *Hikite* position.

At the same time, perform right *Chudan Oi-zuki*.

(side view)

Step forward with the left foot onto left *Zenkutsu-dachi* stance in *Shomen* position.

(side view)

Step forward with the right foot onto right *Zenkutsu-dachi* stance in *Shomen* position.

(side view)

(side view)

At the same time, perform left *Chudan Oi-zuki*.

(side view)

Sequence 5 *Gedan Harai-uke* and *Chudan Oi-zuki* Contd

Step forward with the right foot onto right *Zenkutsu-dachi* stance in *Shomen* position.

(side view)

At the same time, perform right *Chudan Oi-zuki* with *Kiai* (shout).

Sequence 6 *Gedan Shuto-barai*

Pivot on the right foot anti-clockwise through 45 degrees, moving the left foot to the 45 degree line to make *Shiko-dachi* stance in *Ma-hanmi* position.

At the same time, perform left *Gedan Shuto-barai*.

correct position

The *Shuto-barai* movement is identical to that of *Harai-uke*, but with the hand in *Shuto* (knife hand) position instead of a fist. The wrist should be flat (the back of the hand and the forearm should be flat), but with the outer edge of the wrist joint pushed outwards. Remember the fingers should be kept together, not loose, and the hand tensed at the moment of blocking.

(side view)

So, like sequence no.3, the body position should remain at *Shomen* position all the way through this sequence and height should remain the same as well (no bobbing up and down as you step).

Bunkai

Refer to the previous sequence.

wrong positions

The blocking movement should start from the opposite shoulder, which applies to all four *Shuto-barai*s in this sequence. However, the *Hikite* (pulling back of non-blocking hand) movement of the first block is unique. As you have to start the new movement directly from the previous position, which in this case is *Chudan Oi-zuki* position, firstly you should open both hands at *Oi-zuki* position (the right arm extended to the front while the left is pulled back at the side of the body). Then, as you pivot, bring the left hand to the right shoulder. Perform the block from that position at the same time as you fix your stance into *Shiko-dachi* in *Ma-hanmi* position. The right *Shuto* should be placed in front of the solar plexus, palm up and finger tips pointing towards the opponent.

Step forward with the right foot along the same 45 degree line and make right *Shiko-dachi* stance in *Ma-hanmi* position.

At the same time, perform right *Shuto-barai*.

The left *Shuto* should be placed in front of the solar plexus, palm up and finger tips pointing towards the opponent.

At the same time, perform right *Shuto-barai* block. The left *Shuto* remains in front of the solar plexus with minimum movement.

Step forward with the left foot on the same 45 degree line and

make left *Shiko-dachi* stance in *Ma-hanmi* position.

(side view)

Move the right foot towards the 45 degree right line, thus turning clockwise by 90 degrees.

Do not step directly to the right, but first bring the right foot to the side of the left foot before stepping forward.

At the same time, perform left *Shuto-barai* block. The right *Shuto* should be placed in front of the solar plexus, palm up and finger tips pointing towards the opponent.

(side view)

1

Block the opponent's kick with *Shuto-barai*.

2

Step in and strike with *Shuto*.

5

At the same time, throw the opponent down by lifting the kicking leg and pressing down the head.

6

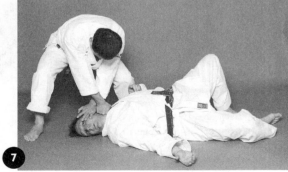

Pin down the head with left hand and punch with the right.

7

3 Move the left foot next to the right foot.

4 Pivot on the left foot, move back the right foot and turn backwards.

Move the left foot back beside the right into *Heiko-dachi* (parallel stance) facing straight forwards and pull back both fists. Keep looking towards the last opponent at 45 degrees right (*Zanshin*).

After a few seconds, look straight forward and push both fists down to *Yoi* position.

First move the right foot in, then the left foot, to make *Musubi-dachi* stance.

At the same time, put both hands together in front of the solar plexus, right hand on top of the left, palms facing upwards.

Then push both hands down to cover the groin (*Naotte* position).

Put both hands to the side of thighs.

Rei (bow)

End of the Kata

Pin'an Shodan

Pin'an Shodan

1

Musubi-dachi

2

Rei (bow)

3

Put both hands in front of the solar plexus (right hand on top, both palms facing upwards).

4

Naotte position (The left hand is outside.)
Here, you should announce the name of the Kata.

Sequence 1 *Jodan Yoko-uke, Chudan Uchi-otoshi* and *Jodan Kentsui-uchi*

Look left and open the right heel.

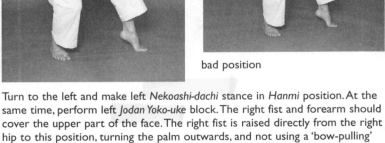

bad position

Turn to the left and make left *Nekoashi-dachi* stance in *Hanmi* position. At the same time, perform left *Jodan Yoko-uke* block. The right fist and forearm should cover the upper part of the face. The right fist is raised directly from the right hip to this position, turning the palm outwards, and not using a 'bow-pulling' action. You should be careful not to raise the right elbow and shoulder.

5 First, open the left foot, change hands to fists and cross arms.

6 Then open the right foot to make *Heiko-dachi* (parallel stance) while pulling back both arms.

7 Lower the fists in front of the groin to make *Yoi* position

Turn hip in to make *Nekoashi-dachi* stance in *Shomen* position. At the same time, perform right inward *Uchi-otoshi* block. The left fist should be pulled back to the right shoulder with elbow down for protection.

Leading with the left foot, slide in to the left, turning the body to make *Heiko-dachi* (parallel stance) in *Ma-hanmi* position. At the same time, perform left *Jodan Kentsui-uchi* (hammer-fist strike). The right fist should be pulled back properly to the side of the body.

Look right.

Then open the left heel and move the right foot slightly to make right *Nekoashi-dachi* stance in *Hanmi* position.

At the same time, perform right *Jodan Yoko-uke* block. The left fist and forearm should cover the upper part of the face.

Do not drop either arm to prepare the block and cover. The block and cover should be performed directly from the previous position.

Bunkai

1

Block the opponent's *Jodan-zuki* with *Yoko-uke*. Right arm covers the face.

2

Block the following *Chudan-zuki* with *Uchi-otoshi* as you turn the body into *Shomen* position. The left arm protects the body.

32

Turn hip forward to make *Nekoashi-dachi* stance in *Shomen* position. At the same time, perform left inward *Uchi-otoshi* block. The right fist should be pulled back to the left shoulder with elbow down for protection.

Leading with the right foot, slide in to the right, turning the body to make *Heiko-dachi* stance in *Ma-hanmi* position. At the same time, perform right *Jodan Kentsui-uchi* strike. The left fist should be pulled back properly to the side of the body.

Slide in and turn the body into *Ma-hanmi* position. At the same time, strike the opponent with *Kentsui-uchi.* The turning of the body together with the slide in adds power to the strike. For that, the hip (or body) should turn towards the target, and should never over-turn.

If the second attack is fairly high (aiming for the chest for example), then you can block from the top, rather than from the side.

Look back over the right shoulder.

Step forward with the left foot, crossing it in front of the right foot.

(side view)

Bunkai

(side views)

When the opponent grabs the shoulder or neck from behind,

(side view)

Pivot on the left foot and turn clockwise to make right *Nekoashi-dachi* stance in *Hanmi* position towards the rear. At the same time, perform right *Chudan Yoko-uke* block. This block should be performed directly from the previous *Kentsui-uchi* position without the fist being lowered down as a preparation.

Then, while keeping the upper-body as it is, perform right *Mae-geri* returning the right foot to make exactly the same *Nekoashi-dachi* stance.

2 step one foot forward, turn briskly and drop the body into *Nekoashi-dachi* stance. At the same time, parry the opponent's grabbing arm with *Yoko-uke* movement.

3 Follow up with *Mae-geri*.

Sequence 3 *Chudan Shuto-uke* and *Chudan Tate-nukite*

(side view)

Look back over the left shoulder, pivot on the ball of the right foot

and turn anti-clockwise 180 degrees to make left *Nekoashi-dachi* stance in *Hanmi* position.

At the same time, perform left *Chudan Shuto-uke* (knife hand block). The right hand is placed in front of the solar plexus, palm up and finger-tips pointing towards the opponent.

Step forward with the left foot on to left *Nekoashi-dachi* stance in *Hanmi* position.

At the same time, perform left *Chudan Shuto-uke* block. The right hand is placed in front of the solar plexus, palm up and finger-tips pointing towards the opponent.

(side view)

Step forward with the right foot on to right *Nekoashi-dachi* stance in *Hanmi* position.

At the same time, perform right *Chudan Shuto-uke* block. The left hand is placed in front of the solar plexus, palm up and finger-tips pointing towards the opponent.

(side view)

Step forward with the right foot on to right *Zenkutsu-dachi* stance in *Shomen* position.

At the same time, perform right *Chudan Tate-nukite* (vertical spear-hand) with *Kiai* (shout). The left hand should make a fist and be pulled back at the side.

Block the opponent's punch with *Shuto-uke*.

With the blocking hand, grab the opponent's wrist and pull. At the same time, counter-attack to the solar plexus with *Tate-nukite*.

Step forward with the right foot on to right *Nekoashi-dachi* stance in *Hanmi* position.

(side view)

At the same time, perform right *Chudan Shuto-uke* block. The left hand is placed in front of the solar plexus, palm up and finger-tips pointing towards the opponent.

Sequence 4 *Chudan Shuto-uke*

(side view)

Pivot on the right foot, moving the left foot, and turn anti-clockwise through 225 degrees to face the 45 degree line and make left *Nekoashi-dachi* stance in *Hanmi* position.

(side view)

At the same time, perform left *Chudan Shuto-uke* block. The right hand is placed in front of the solar plexus, palm up and finger-tips pointing towards the opponent.

(side view)

Move the right foot and turn clockwise through 90 degrees to face the other 45 degree line, and make right *Nekoashi-dachi* stance in *Hanmi* position.

(side view)

At the same time, perform right *Chudan Shuto-uke* block. The left hand remains in front of the solar plexus.

(side view)

Step forward with the left foot on to left *Nekoashi-dachi* stance in *Hanmi* position.

Bunkai

1 Block the opponent's punch with *Shuto-uke*.

2 Grab the opponent's wrist with blocking hand and pull. At the same time, step forward and strike his collar bone with right *Shuto-uchi*.

(front view)

At the same time, perform left *Chudan Shuto-uke* block. The right hand is placed in front of the solar plexus, palm up and the finger-tips pointing towards the opponent.

(side view)

Sequence 5 *Gyaku-hanmi Chudan Yoko-uke, Chudan Mae-geri* and *Chudan Gyaku-zuki*

(front view)

(front view)

Move the left foot, turn anti-clockwise for 45 degrees to face the line directly behind the start position and make left *Zenkutsu-dachi* stance. Twist the upper body to the maximum to make *Gyaku-hanmi* position without losing the stance. At the same time, perform right *Chudan Yoko-uke* block. The left hand should be pulled back at the side in fist position.

Keep the upper body as it is and perform right *Chudan Mae-geri* (front kick).

Sequence 5 *Gyaku-hanmi Chudan Yoko-uke, Chudan Mae-geri* and *Chudan Gyaku-zuki* Contd

(front view)

(front view)

Pull back the kick properly and land forward, making right *Zenkutsu-dachi* stance in *Shomen* position. At the same time, perform left *Chudan Gyaku-zuki* (reverse punch). The right fist should be pulled back to the side.

Keeping the same *Zenkutsu-dachi* stance, twist the upper body to the maximum to make *Gyaku-hanmi* position. At the same time, perform left *Chudan Yoko-uke* block. The right fist remains at the side.

Bunkai

1

2

Avoid the opponent's punch by sliding slightly to the side and twisting the body into *Gyaku-hanmi* position as well as blocking with *Yoko-uke*.

Kick the opponent with *Mae-geri*. If the distance is too close, slide back the front foot accordingly and kick with the back leg.

(front view)

(front view)

Keeping the upper arm as it is, perform left *Chudan Mae-geri*.

Pull back the kick properly and land forward, making left *Zenkutsu-dachi* stance in *Shomen* position. At the same time, perform right *Chudan Gyaku-zuki*. The left fist should be pulled back to the side.

Land forward and follow up with *Chudan Gyaku-zuki*.

Sequence 6 *Chudan Sasae-uke*

(front view)

(front view)

Step forward with the right foot on to *Zenkutsu-dachi* stance in *Shomen* position.

At the same time, perform right *Chudan Sasae-uke* (supported block) with *Kiai* (shout). The bottom of the left fist touches inside the right elbow.

Sequence 7 *Gedan Harai-uke* and *Jodan Age-uke*

Pivot on the right foot, moving the left foot to turn anti-clockwise through 225 degrees to face the 45 degree line, and make left *Zenkutsu-dachi* stance in *Shomen* position.

At the same time, perform left *Gedan Harai-uke* block. The right fist should be pulled back to the side.

Step forward with the right foot on to right *Zenkutsu-dachi* stance in *Shomen* position.

1. Block the opponent's punch with *Sasae-uke*.

2. With the supporting fist, punch the opponent with *Ura-zuki* (reversed fist punch).

At the same time, perform right *Jodan Age-uke* block. The left fist should be pulled back to the side.

Moving the right foot, turn clockwise through 90 degrees to face the other 45 degree line, and make right *Zenkutsu-dachi* stance in *Shomen* position.

At the same time, perform right *Gedan Harai-uke* block. The left fist remains at the side.

Step forward with the left foot on to left *Zenkutsu-dachi* stance in *Shomen* position.

At the same time, perform left *Jodan Age-uke* block. The right fist should be pulled back to the side.

Keep looking towards the last opponent, step back with the left foot and make *Heiko-dachi* stance. At the same time, pull both fists back to the sides. Keep this position for a while (*Zanshin*).

Then look straight forward and push the fists down to cover the groin (*Yoi* position).

First move the right foot in, then the left, to make *Musubi-dachi* stance.

At the same time, put both hands together in front of the solar plexus, right hand on top of the left, palms facing upwards.

Bunkai

1 Block the opponent's punch with *Harai-uke.*

2 Step in and strike the opponent's chin and throat with forearm using *Age-uke* movement.

Then push both hands down to cover the groin (*Naotte* position).

Put both hands to the side of the thighs.

Rei (bow)

End of the Kata

Pin'an Sandan

Pin'an Sandan

1 *Musubi-dachi*

2 *Rei* (bow)

3 Put both hands in front of the solar plexus (right hand on top, both palms facing upwards).

4 *Naotte* position (The left hand is outside.) Here, you should announce the name of the Kata.

Sequence I *Chudan Yoko-uke* and **Morote-uke* (in this case *Yoko-uke* and *Harai-uke* together)

Look left and open the right heel.

Turn to the left and make left *Nekoashi-dachi* stance in *Hanmi* position. At the same time, perform left *Chudan Yoko-uke* block.

Move the right foot forward to the side of the left, still keeping the same height. Bring the right fist to the left hip and the left fist to the right shoulder.

* also known as *Ryo-uke*, meaning any combination of two simultaneous blocks

5 First, open the left foot, change hands to fists and cross arms.

6 Then open the right foot to make *Heiko-dachi* (parallel stance) while pulling back both arms.

7 Lower the fists in front of the groin to make *Yoi* position

As you come up and fix the stance of *Heisoku-dachi*, perform right *Chudan Yoko-uke* and left *Gedan Harai-uke* simultaneously.

Bring the right fist to the left shoulder and the left fist to the right hip.

Perform left *Chudan Yoko-uke* and right *Gedan Harai-uke* simultaneously.

Step left foot forward, in front of the right foot, and look back over the right shoulder. The right fist moves to the left hip.

Pivot on the left foot and turn clockwise and, moving the right foot a little, make right *Nekoashi-dachi* stance in *Hanmi* position. At the same time, perform right *Chudan Yoko-uke* block.

Move the left foot forward to the side of the right, still keeping the same height. Bring the left fist to the right hip and the right fist to the left shoulder.

As you come up and fix the stance of *Heisoku-dachi*, perform left *Chudan Yoko-uke* and right *Gedan Harai-uke* simultaneously.

2 Block the following punch with *Harai-uke* using the same arm. At the same time, strike the opponent with *Ura-uchi* (back fist strike) which is performed in a similar manner to *Yoko-uke*.

3 **Or**; Block the opponent's punch with *Harai-uke* and, at the same time, strike with *Ura-uchi*.

Bring the left fist to the right shoulder and the right fist to the left hip.

Perform right *Chudan Yoko-uke* and left *Gedan Harai-uke* simultaneously.

Block the opponent's punch with *Yoko-uke*.

Same technique can be used against a kick.

Or; Block the opponent's punch with *Yoko-uke* and, at the same time, strike his body or groin with *Kentsui-uchi* (hammer fist strike) in a similar manner to *Harai-uke*.

Sequence 2 *Chudan Yoko-uke* and *Chudan Tate-nukite*

Look left and start turning to the left. At the same time, bring the left fist to the right hip.

Step forward with the left foot and make left *Nekoashi-dachi* stance in *Hanmi* position. At the same time, perform left *Chudan Yoko-uke* block.

Bunkai

Block the opponent's punch with *Yoko-uke*.

(side view)

Step forward with the right foot and make right *Zenkutsu-dachi* stance in *Shomen* position. At the same time, perform right *Chudan Tate-nukite* (vertical spear hand). The left fist is pulled back to the side.

(side view)

Then attack the solar plexus with *Tate-nukite*.

Alternatively, you can attack the throat with *Tate-nukite*.

Sequence 3 *Hikihazushi, Hiji-ate, Kentsui-uchi* and *Chudan Oi-zuki*

Move the left foot slightly to the right so that both feet are aligned. Then shift the stance to right *Kokutsu-dachi*.

As you shift the stance, turn the right *Nukite* 180 degrees anti-clockwise as well as pulling back with the whole body. The right arm should not be bent and upper body is leaning towards the rear slightly.

(side view)

(side view)

Stretch the left arm to strike with *Kentsui-uchi* (hammer fist strike). This and the previous *Hiji-ate* must be performed as one continuous movement.

(side view)

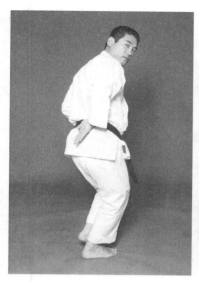

Step back with the left foot. At the same time bend the right elbow so that the back of the turned right hand meets the back of the right hip at the mid-point of the step.

(side view)

Keep moving the left foot, turning the body, and make left *Shiko-dachi* stance in *Ma-hanmi* position. At the same time, perform left *Yoko Hiji-ate* (side elbow strike).

Step forward with the right foot and make *Zenkutsu-dachi* stance in *Shomen* position. At the same time, perform right *Chudan Oi- zuki* with *Kiai* (shout).

(side view)

1 When the opponent grabs your hand or wrist with two hands,

2 shift the stance and pull and twist the arm so that the opponent is stretched forward and slightly off balance.

5

6 Then step across with the back foot, turn and strike the opponent's arm with your elbow, thus disengaging from his grip.

3

Or; If he catches your arm from behind and twists it,

4

make a long step forward with the same side foot and pull the arm so that the opponent is stretched and slightly off balance.

7

Strike his ribs with *Kentsui*.

8

Follow up with punch.

Sequence 4 *Ninoude-uke* and *Chudan Oi-zuki*

Pivot on the right foot to turn anti-clockwise 180 degrees and bring the left foot to the side of the right foot to make *Heisoku-dachi* stance in *Shomen* position. At the same time, bring both fists to the hips, in a position whereby the knuckles face towards the body, palms facing to the rear.

(side view)

Step forward with the right foot then turn sharply to make right *Shiko-dachi* stance in *Ma-hanmi* position.

Follow up immediately with right *Chudan-zuki* from the previous position. Thus the course of the *Tsuki* is different from the normal one.

(side view)

Bring back the punch to the hip straight away (same position as before), making the *Tsuki* quite snappy.

(side view)

At the same time, perform right *Ninoude-uke* (upper arm block). Both fists remain on the hips.

(side view)

(side view)

Step forward with the left foot then turn sharply to make left *Shiko-dachi* stance in *Ma-hanmi* position.

(side view)

Sequence 4 *Ninoude-uke* and *Chudan Oi-zuki* Contd

At the same time, perform left *Ninoude-uke* block. Both fists remain on the hips.

(side view)

Follow up immediately with left *Chudan-zuki.*

(side view)

(side view)

Step forward with the right foot then turn sharply to make right *Shiko-dachi* stance in *Ma-hanmi* position.

At the same time, perform right *Ninoude-uke* block. Both fists remain on the hips.

(side view)

Bring back the punch to the hip straight away (same position as before), making the *Tsuki* quite snappy.

(side view)

(side view)

(side view)

Follow up immediately with right *Chudan-zuki*. This time, the left fist must be pulled back to the side as in normal *Tsuki*, i.e. palm up.

Step forward with the left foot and make left *Zenkutsu-dachi* stance in *Shomen* position.

63

(side view)

At the same time, perform left *Chudan Oi-zuki* with *Kiai* (shout).

Block the opponent's punch with *Ninoude-uke*.

Sequence 5 *Ushiro Hiji-ate* and *Ushiro-zuki*

Bring the right foot forward and make *Heiko-dachi* (or *Shizen-dachi Heiko*, parallel stance).

(side view)

Cross the left foot behind the right, making quite a big step, on to the same line.

Turn anti-clockwise and move the right foot a little so that you are sliding to the side as well as turning, and make *Heiko-dachi* stance.

② Follow up straight away with a punch to the body with the same arm.

③ Followed by a second punch.

(side view)

At the same time, perform left *Ushiro Hiji-ate* (elbow strike towards the rear) and right punch over the left shoulder (*Ushiro-zuki*).

Move the right foot to the right then follow with the left foot, thus sliding to the right, and make *Heiko-dachi*.

At the same time, perform right *Ushiro Hiji-ate* and left punch over the right shoulder (*Ushiro-zuki*).

1 When the attacker holds you from behind,

2 Swing one way with a little slide first and loosen his grip.

3 Then, swing back in the opposite direction and, at the same time, strike his body with your elbow and punch his face.

Then lower the fists to *Yoi* position.

First move the right foot in, then the left foot, to make *Musubi-dachi* stance.

At the same time, put both hands together in front of the solar plexus, right hand on top of the left, palms facing upwards.

Keep looking towards the back over the right shoulder and step forward on the left foot. Both hands remain at the same position.

Then step forward with the right foot to make *Heiko-dachi*. Keep looking towards the last opponent for a while (*Zanshin*).

Look forward and pull back the left fist to the side.

Then push both hands down to cover the groin (*Naotte* position).

Put both hands to the side of thighs.

Rei (bow)

End of the Kata

Pin'an Yondan

Pin'an Yondan

1

Musubi-dachi

2

Rei (bow)

3

Put both hands in front of the solar plexus (right hand on top, both palms facing upwards).

4

Naotte position (The left hand is outside.)
Here, you should announce the name of the Kata.

Sequence 1 *Jodan Haishu-uke* (back of hand block)

Look left and open the right heel.

Make left *Nekoashi-dachi* (cat stance) in Hanmi position.

At the same time, perform left *Jodan Haishu-uke* block. The right open hand and forearm should cover the upper part of the face. This is a very similar movement to the first movement of *Pin'an Shodan*, only the hands are open and the angle of the front forearm (degree of twist) is slightly different.

5

First, open the left foot, change hands to fists and cross arms.

6

Then open the right foot to make *Heiko-dachi* (parallel stance) while pulling back both arms.

7

Lower the fists in front of the groin to make *Yoi* position

Look back and pivot on the ball of the left foot and start opening the left heel.

Turn 180 degrees clockwise and make right *Nekoashi-dachi* stance in *Hanmi* position. At the same time, perform right *JodanHaishu-uke*. The left open hand and forearm should cover the upper part of the face. You should perform this block from the previous position (left *Haishu-uke*) without lowering the arms too much.

1

Block the opponent's punch with *Haishu-uke*. The other hand protects the face and head.

Grab the opponent's punching arm with your blocking hand and pull him off balance. At the same time, strike his neck with *Shuto-uchi* (knife hand strike).

While blocking the opponent's kick with left *Gedan Harai-uke*, punch the shin of the kicking leg with the right vertical fist (*Tateken*), punching slightly from the side.

Sequence 3 *Chudan Sasae-uke* (supported block)

Step forward with the right foot and make right *Nekoashi-dachi* stance in *Hanmi* position.

At the same time, perform right *Chudan Sasae-uke*. Left *Kentsui* (bottom of fist) supports the inside of the right elbow.

Sequence 2 *Gedan Kosa-uke* (cross block)

(close up)

Look left and bring the left foot near the right. At the same time, bring both fists to the right hip, the right fist on top of the left with the backs of the hands facing each other (the left is pointing right and the right is pointing forwards).

Step forward with the left foot and make left *Zenkutsu-dachi* stance in *Shomen* position. At the same time, perform *Gedan Kosa-uke*, right arm on top of the left.

i.e. the left arm performs *Gedan Harai-uke* block, whereas the right is actually a vertical fist punch (*Tateken-zuki*) downwards.

Bunkai

Block the opponent's punch with *Chudan Sasae-uke*.

While controlling the opponent with the blocking arm, punch with the supporting arm.

Or, grab and pull the opponent's punching arm with the supporting hand and punch with the blocking arm.

Sequence 4 *Yoko-barai* (side sweeping block), *Yoko-geri* (side kick) and *Chudan Mawashi Hiji-ate* (or *Empi*, [round house elbow strike])

Move left foot forward next to the right foot and make *Heisoku-dachi* stance. At the same time, bring both fists to the right hip, the left fist on top of the right with palms facing each other.

Look left and perform left *Yoko-barai* and *Yoko-geri* consecutively.

This *Yoko-geri* is not a long thrusting kick. It is rather a short sharp snappy one.

Move the right foot next to the left, turn clockwise through 90 degrees to face the front and make *Heisoku-dachi* stance. At the same time, bring both fists to the left hip, right fist on top of the left and palms facing each other.

Look right and perform right *Yoko-barai* and *Yoko-geri* consecutively.

These should be done in exactly the same manner as the left side.

While keeping the blocking arm in position, pull back (or snap back) the kick quickly.

As you land with the left foot, push the right leg and turn the body sharply to make left *Zenkutsu-dachi* stance in *Shomen* position.

At the same time, perform right *Chudan Mawashi Hiji-ate* on the left palm which is pulled back quickly from the blocking position.

As you land with the right foot, push the left leg and turn the body sharply to make *Zenkutsu-dachi* stance in *Shomen* position.

At the same time, perform left *Chudan Mawashi Hiji-ate* on the right palm which is pulled back quickly from the blocking position.

1 Block the opponent's punch with *Yoko-barai*.

2 Grab the punching arm and pull as you kick with *Yoko-geri*.

Sequence 5 *Gedan Shotei Harai-uke* (palm heel sweeping block), *Jodan Sukui-uke* (scooping block)

* NOTE

Although we perform snappy *Yoko-geri* at this part of the Kata, the original version is with *Mae-geri* (front kick) as seen in *Kosokun* Katas. In view of the fact that the *Yoko-geri* version is quite widely practised within *Tani-ha Shito-ryu* as seen in Master Tani's book, we chose this version as our standardised version so that students get the opportunity to practise this type of *Yoko-geri*.

Look left and perform left *Gedan Shotei Harai-uke* block with the right hand covering the head. The stance is unchanged.

Push the right leg and shift the stance on the spot to make left *Sokkutsu-dachi*. The body is turned to *Ma-hanmi* position. At the same time, perform right *Jodan Sukui-uke* with the left hand covering the head.

3

As you pull him further to upset his balance, strike with *Mawashi Hiji-ate* (elbow strike).

4

Alternatively, hold the back of his head or neck and pull him down as you strike his face with *Mawashi Hiji-ate*.

Chudan Mae-geri (front kick), *Shotei Osae-uke* (palm heel pressing down block) and *Jodan Ura-uchi* (back fist strike)

Perform right *Mae-geri* (front kick). Make sure the hand positions are unchanged as you do it.

As you land forward with the right foot after pulling back the kick, perform left *Shotei Osae-uke*. The right fist comes inside to protect the body.

As you move the left foot behind the right to make *Kosa-dachi* (cross stance), perform right *Ura-uchi* with *Kiai* (shout). The left hand must be pulled back to the side in a fist. The body position is almost *Ma-hanmi* position.

1 Block the opponent's kick with *Shotei Harai-uke*.

2 Block the following punch with both hands. With the left, catch the wrist and turn it, while the right *Sukui-uke* applies pressure on the elbow.

4 Pull the opponent's arm near the shoulder with the left hand as you land the kicking foot, then strike his face with *Ura-uchi* as you cross the rear leg and make *Kosa-dachi*.

3 While keeping the pressure on the elbow, kick the opponent with *Mae-geri*.

5 Turn round and throw the opponent with *Ippon-seoi-nage* (one-arm over-the-shoulder throw) or *Tai-otoshi* (body-drop throw).

6 Punch or kick the opponent to finish off.

79

Sequence 6 *Yoko-uke, Mae-geri* and *Niren-zuki* (double punches or consecutive punches)

(front view)

(front view)

Pivot on the right foot and move the left foot to turn anti-clockwise through 225 degrees to face the left 45 degree line and make left *Nekoashi-dachi* in *Hanmi* position. At the same time, perform left *Chudan Yoko-uke* block.

Perform right *Chudan Mae-geri*.

(front view)

(front view)

Move the right foot and turn clockwise 90 degrees to face the right 45 degree line and make right *Nekoashi-dachi* in *Hanmi* position. At the same time, perform right *Chudan Yoko-uke* block.

Perform left *Chudan Mae-geri*.

(front view)

(front view)

Land forward and push the back leg to make right *Zenkutsu-dachi* stance in *Shomen* position.

At the same time, perform right and then left *Chudan-zuki* consecutively - *Niren-zuki*.

(front view)

(front view)

As you land forward, push the right leg and make left *Zenkutsu-dachi* stance in *Shomen* position.

At the same time, perform left then right *Chudan-zuki* consecutively – *Niren-zuki*.

1 Block the opponent's punch with *Yoko-uke*.

2 Kick the opponent with *Mae-geri*

Sequence 7 *Chudan Sasae-uke* (supported block)

(front view)

(front view)

Move the left foot and turn anti-clockwise through 45 degrees, and make left *Nekoashi-dachi* stance in *Hanmi* position. You are now following a line to the rear of the start position.

At the same time, perform left *Chudan Sasae-uke* block with right *Kentsui* (bottom of fist) supporting the inside of the left elbow.

3

As you land forward, punch the opponent with *Niren-zuki*.

4

(front view)

Step forward with the right foot and make right *Nekoashi-dachi* stance in *Hanmi* position.

(front view)

At the same time, perform right *Chudan Sasae-uke* block.

Sequence 7 *Chudan Sasae-uke* (supported block) *Contd*

(front view)

(front view)

Step forward with the left foot and make left *Nekoashi-dachi* stance in *Hanmi* position.

At the same time, perform left *Chudan Sasae-uke* block.

Bunkai

Refer to sequence 3.

Bunkai

1

Example A. Block the opponent's punch with *Chudan Sasae-uke*.

2

Punch the opponent with the supporting arm.

Sequence 8 *Hiza-geri* (knee kick)

(front view)

As you turn the body into *Shomen* position from *Sasae-uke* position, extend both arms to catch the opponent.

(front view)

Grab the opponent at shoulder height and pull down as you kick with *Hiza-geri* (knee kick) with *Kiai* (shout). As you kick with the knee, you should stretch the ankle of the kicking leg. Note closed fists at the finish of the pulling action.

3 Catch the opponent by the back of the neck.

4 Pull him down and kick with knee.

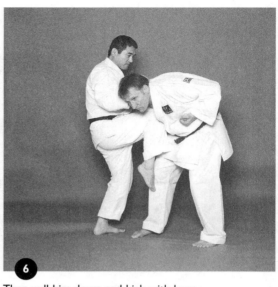

Example B Alternatively, you can hook the opponent's neck as well as catching the punching arm.

Then pull him down and kick with knee.

Turn clockwise through 90 degrees to face right 45 degree line. Step in with the right foot, heel first, changing to the ball of the foot as you bring the left foot forward to make right *Nekoashi-dachi* stance in *Hanmi* position.

As the left foot moves forward to follow the right, perform right *Chudan Shuto-uke* block. The left hand covers the solar plexus with the palm facing upwards.

Sequence 9 *Shuto-uke* (knife hand block)

After the knee kick, land straight forward.

Pivot on the right foot and, moving the left foot, turn anti-clockwise through 225 degrees to face left 45 degree line and make left *Nekoashi-dachi* stance in *Hanmi* position.

At the same time, perform left *Chudan Shuto-uke*. The right hand covers the solar plexus with the palm facing upwards.

Bunkai

Example A Block the opponent's punch with *Shuto-uke*.

Follow up with *Maeashi-geri* (front leg kick).

3 **Example B** Avoid the opponent's punch.

4 Stamp the instep of the opponent's front foot with heel.

Slide back left foot followed by right foot to make *Heiko-dachi* (parallel stance) and pull back both fists to the sides.

Keep looking towards the last opponent at 45 degrees right for a while (*Zanshin*).

Look forward and lower fists to *Yoi* position.

First move the right foot in, then the left foot, to make *Musubi-dachi* stance.

5 Move the back foot forward to make *Nekoashi-dachi* stance. At the same time, strike the opponent's upper arm or shoulder to put him off balance.

6 Follow up with *Maeashi-geri*.

At the same time, put both hands together in front of the solar plexus, right hand on top of the left, palms facing upwards.

Then push both hands down to cover the groin (*Naotte* position).

Put both hands to the side of thighs.

Rei (bow)

End of the Kata

Pin'an Godan

Pin'an Godan

1 *Musubi-dachi*

2 *Rei* (bow)

3 Put both hands in front of the solar plexus (right hand on top, both palms facing upwards).

4 *Naotte* position (The left hand is outside.)
Here, you should announce the name of the Kata.

Sequence I *Chudan Yoko-uke* and *Chudan Gyaku-zuki*

Look left, open right heel and start turning to the left.

Make left *Nekoashi-dachi** stance and perform left *Chudan Yoko-uke* block.

Follow up with right *Chudan Gyaku-zuki* (reverse punch).

* Although you can block in *Hanmi Nekoashi-dachi* stance and then change to *Shomen* position and punch, it is easier and probably better to block already in *Shomen Nekoashi-dachi* stance and follow up straight away with *Gyaku-zuki*.

5 First, open the left foot, change hands to fists and cross arms.

6 Then open the right foot to make *Heiko-dachi* (parallel stance) while pulling back both arms.

7 Lower the fists in front of the groin to make *Yoi* position

Move the right foot forward and turn clockwise through 90 degrees and make *Heisoku-dachi* stance facing front. At the same time, pull both fists to the right hip, left on top and palms facing each other.

Look right and place the right foot to the right.

Make right *Nekoashi-dachi** stance and perform right *Chudan Yoko-uke* block.

* see note for left hand side

Follow up with left *Chudan Gyaku-zuki.*

93

Move the left foot forward and turn anti-clockwise through 90 degrees and make *Heisoku-dachi* stance facing front. At the same time, pull both fists to the left hip, right on top and palms facing each other.

Block the opponent's punch with *Chudan Yoko-uke*.

Sequence 2 *Chudan Sasae-uke* (supported block)

Step forward with the right foot and make right *Moto-dachi* stance in *Shomen* position. At the same time, perform right *Chudan Sasae-uke* block. Left *Kentsui* (bottom of fist) supports the inside of the right elbow.

(side view)

Refer to '*Pinan Yondan*', sequence 3.

Counter attack with *Chudan Gyaku-zuki*.

Hold the opponent's punching fist with two hands. Twist and pull to the right hip.

Sequence 3 *Gedan Kosa-uke* (cross block)

As you start to step forward with the left foot, bring both fists to the right hip with right fist on top and the backs of the hands facing each other.

Step forward with the left foot and make left *Zenkutsu-dachi* stance in *Shomen* position. At the same time, perform *Gedan Kosa-uke* block with right arm on top of the left, i.e. the left arm performs *Gedan Harai-uke* block whereas the right is a vertical fist (*Tateken-zuki*) punch downwards.

* Refer to '*Pin'an Yondan*' sequence 2.

Sequence 4 *Jodan Kosa-uke, Gyaku-waza, Kentsui-uchi* and *Chudan Oi-zuki*

Bring both fists to the chest, still crossed.

Keeping the arms still crossed, open hands and block upwards and slightly forwards with both arms (*Jodan Kosa-uke*).

Rolling both hands inwards as you bring them down to the right hip,

at the same time, move the right foot slightly and shift stance into *Shiko-dachi* in *Ma-hanmi* position.

(side view)

Step forward with the right foot and make right *Zenkutsu-dachi* in *Shomen* position.

(side view)

At the same time, perform right *Chudan Oi-zuki*.

(side view)

Strike with left *Kentsui* (bottom of fist) at shoulder height. As you strike, the right hand must be closed into fist.

(side view)

Bunkai (sequences 3 & 4)

1

Block the opponent's kick with *Harai-uke*. At the same time, punch his shin.

2

Block the following punch with *Jodan Kosa-uke*.

B u n k a i (sequences 3 & 4)

3 Grab his wrist with the left hand and roll down and pull towards the right hip twisting his arm, and put pressure on his elbow joint with left elbow.

Sequence 5 *Gedan Harai-uke* and *Yoko-barai*

Pivot on the left foot and turn anti-clockwise, step back with the right foot and make right *Shiko-dachi* stance in *Ma-hanmi* position. (Your feet move along one line but your body turns through 270 degrees.)

(side view)

At the same time, perform right *Gedan Harai-uke* block with the left arm covering in front of, and parallel to, the body at solar plexus height.

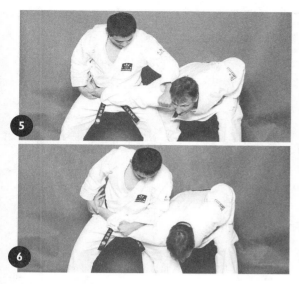

Strike his head with *Kentsui-uchi*.

Give more pressure to the elbow joint,

and punch the head.

(side view)

Look back and move the right foot to the left to make left *Heiko-dachi* (or *Shizen-dachi Heiko*, parallel stance) in *Ma-hanmi* position. At the same time, perform left *Yoko-barai* block. The right fist must be pulled to the side.

(side view)

1 Block the opponent's kick with *Gedan Harai-uke* as you drop and turn the body into *Shiko-dachi* stance. At the same time (or straight after), punch his stomach with *Chudan Kagi-zuki* (hook punch).

2 Step forward with the back foot and strike with *Kentsui*. At the same time, scoop up the opponent's kicking leg with your blocking arm. In most cases, this action should be enough to throw him down to the floor. Otherwise, sweep or hook his supporting leg with either leg.

(side view)

Cross the left leg behind the right and make *Kosa-dachi* stance in *Hanmi* position. At the same time, perform right *Ura-uchi* (back fist strike) with *Kiai* (shout). This strike action should proceed directly from the previous elbow strike position. The left hand should be closed to make a fist and supports the right elbow underneath with the palm facing downwards. The right foot points straight forward and the left makes a right angle to it. Most of the body weight should be supported by the right leg.

Sequence 6 *Mawashi Hiji-ate* and *Ura-uchi*

(side view)

(side view)

Step forward with the right foot and make *Moto-dachi* stance in *Shomen* position.

At the same time, perform right *Mawashi Hiji-ate* (roundhouse elbow strike) on the left palm which should be opened in vertical position and pulled back to meet the elbow.

Bunkai

1 Block the opponent's punch with *Yoko-barai*.

2 Catch the punching arm and step in to strike with *Mawashi Hiji-ate*.

3

As you place the back foot behind the front foot to make *Kosa-dachi* stance, strike the opponent with *Ura-uchi* (back fist strike).

4

Move the back foot further back, then shift stance from one side to the other to throw the opponent with *Tai-otoshi* (body drop throw).

Sequence 7 Jump and *Gedan Kosa-uke*

(side view)

Note

From the previous position, look back and step back with the left foot to make left *Kokutsu-dachi* stance. This *Kokutsu-dachi* is slightly different from the usual *Kokutsu-dachi* where the front leg and hip are locked. Note that the position of *Ura-uchi* and the supporting arm relative to the body is unchanged.

Kokutsu-dachi with locked front leg and hip.
Do not lock them in this position.

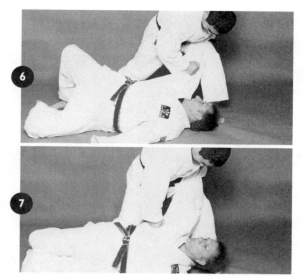

Finish off with punch or kick.

(side view)

(front view)

Lift the right foot, turn the body anti-clockwise through 180 degrees and jump up by pushing off with the left leg. Height is more important than the length of the jump.

While in the air, bend both legs to have a good space underneath.

(front view)

As you land, cross the left foot behind the right. Both knees should be bent well to make a low stance. Keep the upper body relatively upright. At the same time, perform *Gedan Kosa-uke* block. Make sure both fists are pulled back to the hips as part of the blocking process.

Example A As the opponent sweeps your legs with a baton (or staff), avoid it by jumping up with legs bent.

Finish off by punching to the head.

Example B Alternatively, you can use this footwork without the jump element to avoid the opponent's punch and throw him by catching his arm and back of the neck.

2

As you land hold the opponent's shoulder or upper arm.

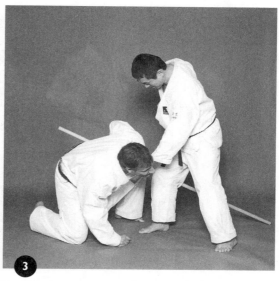

3

By using the momentum of crossing the back leg behind, pull the opponent off balance.

6

7

Finish off with a punch or kick.

Sequence 8 *Chudan Sasae-uke*

Step forward with the right foot and make right *Zenkutsu-dachi* in *Shomen* position. At the same time, perform right *Chudan Sasae-uke* block with *Kiai* (shout). The bottom of the left fist supports the inside of the right elbow.

(front view)

Refer to '*Pin'an Yondan*' sequence 3.

Or, specific to this kata, From the previous position,

Sequence 9 *Harai-uke* and *Yoko-uke* in *Kokutsu-dachi*

Pivot on the right foot and turn anti-clockwise through 225 degrees moving the left foot to face the left 45 degree line in semi-*Zenkutsu-dachi* stance (almost like *Zenkutsu-dachi*, but do not fix the stance). The right fist is extended forward and downwards with the palm facing upwards, while the left is placed at the right shoulder.

Shift the stance into *Kokutsu-dachi*, locking the left leg and hip. At the same time, perform left *Gedan Harai-uke* and right *Jodan Yoko-uke* blocks (the right fist is at ear height). Both blocks and the body must be aligned in one line.

hold the opponent's lapel (or hair) with the punching hand and pull him off balance in the opposite direction using the step of the front foot.

Finish off with *Ura-zuki*.

Bring the left foot back next to the right in a smooth movement. Do not get higher, keep the same height.

Step with the right foot to the right 45 degree line in semi-*Zenkutsu-dachi* stance. The left fist is extended forward and downwards with palm facing upwards, while the right is placed at the left shoulder.

Shift the stance into *Kokutsu-dachi*, locking the right leg and hip. At the same time, perform right *Gedan Harai-uke* and left *Jodan Yoko-uke* blocks (the left fist is at ear height). Both blocks and the body should be aligned in one line.

Example A Avoid the opponent's kick by shifting stance into *Kokutsu- dachi.* As you avoid the kick, block the kick away with *Harai-uke* using the quick turn of the body and fixation to produce a snappy effect. The back hand pulled back in *Yoko-uke* manner helps this action.

Shift back the stance and project forward to punch.

Strike the groin, which has been opened up by the previous action, with *Kentsui.*

Bring the right foot back to make *Heiko-dachi* (or *Shizen-dachi Heiko*) facing the front. At the same time, pull back both fists to the sides. Keep looking towards the last opponent for a while (*Zanshin*).

Example B Block the opponent's punch with *Jodan Yoko-uke*.

Step with the front foot inside the front leg of the opponent into *Kokutsu-dachi* position. This action will effectively sweep the opponent's front leg, thus putting him off balance.

Look straight forward and bring both fists down to cover the groin (*Yoi* position).

First move the right foot in, then the left foot, to make *Musubi-dachi* stance.

At the same time, put both hands together in front of the solar plexus, right hand on top of the left, palms facing upwards.

Then push both hands down to cover the groin (*Naotte* position).

Put both hands to the side of thighs.

Rei (bow)

End of the Kata

Heian Katas

Heian Nidan

Musubi-dachi

Open the right foot to the right and make *Hachiji-dachi* (or *Soto-hachiji-dachi*) stance. Both fists are placed in front of thighs.

Pivot on the right foot and turn to the left. Move the left foot a little and make left *Nekoashi-dachi* stance. At the same time, swing the left arm anti-clockwise and block to the left. The left arm should be kept fairly straight and the block must stop at shoulder height. The right fist is pulled to the side.

Pivot on the right foot and, moving to the left, turn anti-clockwise through 90 degrees to face the front. Make left *Zenkutsu-dachi* stance and, at the same time, perform left *Gedan Harai-uke* block. The right fist remains at the side.

Step forward with the right foot and make right *Zenkutsu-dachi* stance. At the same time, perform right *Jodan Age-uke* block. Pull back the left fist to the side.

Step forward with the left foot and make left *Zenkutsu-dachi* stance. At the same time, perform left *Jodan Age-uke* block. Pull back the right fist to the side.

Step forward with the right foot and make right *Zenkutsu-dachi* stance. At the same time, perform right *Jodan Age-uke* block. Pull back the left fist to the side.

Step forward with the right foot and make right *Moto-dachi* stance. At the same time, perform right *Chudan Oi-zuki*. The left fist is pulled to the side.

Step back with the right foot and turn clockwise through 180 degrees to face the other way. Make right *Zenkutsu-dachi* stance and, at the same time, perform right *Gedan Harai-uke* block. The left fist remains at the side.

Move back the right foot a little and change stance to right *Moto-dachi*. At the same time, swing the right arm clockwise to block. The right arm should be kept fairly straight and the block must stop at shoulder height. The left fist remains at the side.

Step forward with the left foot and make left *Moto-dachi* stance. At the same time, perform left *Chudan Oi-zuki*. The right fist is pulled to the side.

Pivot on the right foot and, moving to the left, turn anti-clockwise through 225 degrees to face the left 45 degree line. Make left *Zenkutsu-dachi* stance and, at the same time, perform left *Gedan Harai-uke* block. The right fist is pulled back to the side.

Step forward with the right foot and make right *Moto-dachi* stance. At the same time, perform right *Chudan Oi-zuki*. The left fist is pulled back to the side.

Move the right foot and turn clockwise through 90 degrees to face the right 45 degree line. Make right *Zenkutsu-dachi* stance and, at the same time, perform right *Gedan Harai-uke* block. The left fist remains at the side.

Step forward with the left foot and make left *Moto-dachi* stance. At the same time, perform left *Chudan Oi-zuki*. The right fist is pulled back to the side.

Move the left foot and turn anti-clockwise through 45 degrees to face the rear. Make left *Zenkutsu-dachi* stance and, at the same time, perform left *Gedan Harai-uke* block. The right fist remains at the side.

(side view)

Step forward with the right foot and make right *Moto-dachi* stance. At the same time, perform right *Chudan Oi-zuki*. The left fist is pulled back to the side.

(side view)

Pivot on the right foot and move the left to turn anti-clockwise through 225 degrees to face the left 45 degree line. Make *Shiko-dachi* stance in *Ma-hanmi* position and, at the same time, perform left *Shuto-barai* block. The right open hand (*Shuto*) is pulled back to the front of the solar plexus with the palm facing upwards.

Step forward with the right foot along the left 45 degree line and make *Shiko-dachi* stance in *Ma-hanmi* position. At the same time, perform right *Shuto-barai* block. The left open hand is pulled back to the front of the solar plexus with the palm facing upwards.

Step forward with the left foot and make left *Moto-dachi* stance. At the same time, perform left *Chudan Oi-zuki*. The right fist is pulled back to the side.

(side view)

Step forward with the right foot and make right *Moto-dachi* stance. At the same time, perform right *Chudan Oi-zuki*. The left fist is pulled back to the side.

(side view)

Move right foot and turn clockwise through 90 degrees and make *Shiko-dachi* stance in *Ma-hanmi* position on the right 45 degree line. At the same time, perform right *Shuto-barai* block. The left hand is moved slightly and re-pulled back to the front of the solar plexus with the palm facing upwards.

Step forward with the left foot along the right 45 degree line and make *Shiko-dachi* stance in *Ma-hanmi* position. At the same time, perform left *Shuto-barai* block. The right open hand is pulled back to the front of the solar plexus with the palm facing upwards.

Move back the left foot and make *Hachiji-dachi* (or *Soto-hachiji-dachi*) stance in *Shomen* position towards the front. Bring the fists in front of thighs. Keep looking towards the last opponent at the right 45 degree direction for a period of one breath (*Zanshin*), then look forward.

Move the right foot and make *Musubi-dachi* stance and bring hands to the sides of the thighs.

End of the Kata

Heian Shodan

Musubi-dachi

Open the right foot to the right and make *Hachiji-dachi* (or *Soto-hachiji-dachi*) stance. Both fists are placed in front of thighs.

Pivot on the right foot and turn to the left. Move the left foot a little and make left *Nekoashi-dachi* stance. At the same time, perform left *Chudan Yoko-uke* block. The right fist and forearm should cover the side of the head.

Remain in *Nekoashi-dachi* stance and perform right inward *Uchi-otoshi* block. The left fist should be pulled back to the right shoulder with elbow down.

Pivot on the left foot clockwise through 90 degrees and perform right *Chudan Yoko-uke* block and *Chudan Mae-geri* kick at the same time.

Land the kicking foot in front and pivot on it to turn anti-clockwise through 180 degrees. Face front and make left *Nekoashi-dachi* stance. At the same time, perform left *Chudan Shuto-uke* block. The right hand should be pulled back in front of the solar plexus with the palm facing upwards.

Step forward with the right foot and make right *Nekoashi-dachi* stance. At the same time, perform right *Chudan Shuto-uke* block. The left hand is pulled back in front of the solar plexus with the palm facing upwards.

Step forward with the left foot and make left *Nekoashi-dachi* stance. At the same time, perform left *Chudan Shuto-uke* block. The right hand is pulled back in front of the solar plexus with the palm facing upwards.

Slide in and turn the body to make *Hachiji-dachi* (*Soto-hachiji-dachi*) in *Ma-hanmi* position. At the same time, perform left *Kentsui-uchi* (hammer fist strike) at shoulder height. The right fist should be pulled back to the side of the body.

Pivot on the left foot and turn back clockwise. Make right *Nekoashi-dachi* and perform right *Chudan Yoko-uke* block. The left fist and forearm should cover the side of the head.

Remain in *Nekoashi-dachi* stance and perform left inward *Uchi-otoshi* block. The right fist should be pulled back to the left shoulder with elbow down.

Slide in and turn the body to make *Hachiji-dachi* (*Soto-hachiji-dachi*) in *Ma-hanmi* position. At the same time, perform right *Kentsui-uchi* (hammer fist strike) at shoulder height. The left fist should be pulled back to the side of the body.

Step forward with the right foot and make right *Moto-dachi* stance. At the same time, perform right *Chudan Tate-nukite* (vertical spear hand). The left fist should be pulled back to the side.

Pivot on the right foot and turn anti-clockwise through 225 degrees to face left 45 degree line. Make left *Nekoashi-dachi* stance and, at the same time, perform left *Chudan Shuto-uke* block. The right hand is pulled back in front of the solar plexus with the palm facing upwards.

Step forward with the right foot and make right *Nekoashi-dachi* stance. At the same time, perform right *Chudan Shuto-uke* block. The left hand is pulled back in front of the solar plexus.

Move the right foot and turn clockwise through 90 degrees to face right 45 degree line. Make right *Nekoashi-dachi* stance and, at the same time, perform right *Chudan Shuto-uke* block. The left hand is placed in front of the solar plexus.

Step forward with the left foot and make left *Nekoashi-dachi* stance. At the same time, perform left *Chudan Shuto-uke* block. The right hand is pulled back in front of the solar plexus.

Move the left foot and turn anti-clockwise through 45 degrees to face the rear. Make left *Moto-dachi* stance and, at the same time, perform right *Chudan Yoko-uke* block. The left fist is pulled back to the side.

(side view)

Keeping the upper body as it is, perform right *Chudan Mae-geri*.

(side view)

Keeping the upper body as it is, perform left *Chudan Mae-geri*.

(side view)

Land forward and make left *Moto-dachi* stance. At the same time, perform right *Chudan Gyaku-zuki*. The left fist is pulled back to the side.

(side view)

Land forward and make right *Moto-dachi* stance. At the same time, perform left *Chudan Gyaku-zuki*. The right fist is pulled back to the side.

(side view)

Keeping the same stance, turn hip and perform left *Chudan Yoko-uke* block. The right fist remains at the side.

(side view)

Step forward with the right foot and make right *Zenkutsu-dachi* stance. At the same time, perform right *Chudan Sasae-uke* (supported block). The left bottom fist is placed inside the right elbow.

(side view)

Pivot on the right foot and turn anti-clockwise through 225 degrees to face the left 45 degree line. Make left *Zenkutsu-dachi* stance and, at the same time, perform left *Gedan Harai-uke* block. The right fist is pulled back to the side.

Step forward with the right foot and make right *Zenkutsu-dachi* stance. At the same time, perform right *Jodan Age-uke* block. The left fist is pulled back to the side.

Move the right foot and turn clockwise through 90 degrees to face the right 45 degree line. Make right *Zenkutsu-dachi* stance and, at the same time, perform right *Gedan Harai-uke* block. The left fist remains at the side.

Step forward with the left foot and make left *Zenkutsu-dachi* stance. At the same time, perform left *Jodan Age-uke* block. The right fist is pulled back to the side.

Move back the left foot and make *Hachiji-dachi* (or *Soto-hachiji-dachi*) stance in *Shomen* position towards the front. Bring the fists in front of thighs. Keep looking towards the last opponent at the right 45 degree direction for a period of one breath (*Zanshin*), then look forward.

Move the right foot and make *Musubi-dachi* stance and bring hands to the sides of the thighs.

End of the Kata

Heian Sandan

Musubi-dachi

Open the right foot to the right and make *Hachiji-dachi* (or *Soto-hachiji-dachi*) stance. Both fists are placed in front of thighs.

Pivot on the right foot and turn to the left. Move the left foot a little and make left *Nekoashi-dachi* stance. At the same time, perform left *Chudan Yoko-uke* block. The right fist is pulled back to the side.

Move the right foot next to the left and make *Musubi-dachi* stance. At the same time, perform right *Chudan Yoko-uke* block and left *Gedan Harai-uke* block simultaneously.

Move the left foot and turn anti-clockwise through 90 degrees to make left *Nekoashi-dachi* stance. At the same time, perform left *Chudan Yoko-uke* block. The right fist is pulled back to the side.

(side view)

Step forward with the right foot and make right *Moto-dachi* stance. At the same time, perform right *Chudan Tate-nukite* (vertical spear hand). The left fist is pulled back to the side.

(side view)

On the same spot, perform left *Chudan Yoko-uke* block and right *Gedan Harai-uke* block simultaneously.

Turn clockwise through 180 degrees and move the right foot to make right *Nekoashi-dachi* stance. At the same time, perform right *Chudan Yoko-uke* block. The left fist is pulled back to the side.

Move the left foot next to the right and make *Musubi-dachi* stance. At the same time, perform left *Chudan Yoko-uke* block and right *Gedan Harai-uke* block simultaneously.

On the same spot, perform right *Chudan Yoko-uke* block and left *Gedan Harai-uke* block simultaneously.

Advance the right foot a little and turn the body anti-clockwise to make right *Kokutsu-dachi* stance. At the same time, pull and turn the right hand so that the back of the hand touches the right hip.

(side view)

Step forward with the left foot and make side facing *Shiko-dachi* stance. At the same time, perform left *Yoko-barai* at shoulder height. The right fist is pulled back to the side.

(side view)

Step forward with the right foot and make right *Moto-dachi* stance. At the same time, perform right *Chudan Oi-zuki*. The left fist is pulled back to the side.

(side view)

Pivot on the right foot and turn anti-clockwise through 180 degrees to face the rear. Bring the left foot next to the right and make *Musubi-dachi* stance. Both fists are placed at the hips with the palms facing back.

(side view)

Step forward with the left foot and make *Shiko-dachi* stance. At the same time, push the left elbow to the level of the front line of the stomach.

(side view)

Perform left *Chudan-zuki* directly from the previous position. Bring the fist back to the hip straight away.

(side view)

Step forward with the right foot and make *Shiko-dachi* stance. At the same time, push the right elbow to the level of the front line of the stomach. This represents a block (*Ninoude-uke*): do not over-block.

(side view)

Perform right *Chudan-zuki* directly from the previous position. Bring the fist back to the hip straight away.

(side view)

Step forward with the right foot and make *Shiko-dachi* stance. At the same time, push the right elbow to the level of the front line of the stomach.

(side view)

Perform right *Chudan-zuki* directly from the previous position. This time, hold the fist at the punching position without bringing it back.

(side view)

Step forward with the left foot and make left *Moto-dachi* stance. At the same time, perform left *Chudan Oi-zuki*. The right fist is pulled back to the side.

(side view)

Keeping the upper body as it is, move the right foot forward to make *Hachiji-dachi* (*Soto-hachiji-dachi*) stance.

Pivot on the right foot and move the left to turn anti-clockwise through 180 degrees to make *Hachiji-dachi* (*Soto-hachiji-dachi*) stance. At the same time, perform left elbow strike towards the rear and right punch over the shoulder towards the rear simultaneously.

Slide to the right (move the right foot then the left) and, at the same time, perform right elbow strike towards the rear and left punch over the shoulder towards the rear simultaneously. The stance remains the same.

Slide to the left (move the left foot then the right) and bring the fists in front of the thighs. The stance is still the same.

Move the right foot and make *Musubi-dachi* stance and bring hands to the sides of the thighs.

End of the Kata

Musubi-dachi

Open the right foot to the right and make *Hachiji-dachi* (or *Soto-hachiji-dachi*) stance. Both fists are placed in front of thighs.

Pivot on the right foot and turn to the left. Move the left foot a little and make left *Nekoashi-dachi* stance. At the same time, perform left *Chudan Haishu-uke* block. The right hand should cover the side of the head.

Turn clockwise through 180 degrees and make right *Nekoashi-dachi* stance. At the same time, perform right *Chudan Haishu-uke* block. The left hand should cover the side of the head.

Land forward and make left *Zenkutsu-dachi* stance. At the same time, open the left hand and bring it in front of the body and strike it with right *Hiji-ate* (elbow strike).

Bring the right foot next to the left and make *Heisoku-dachi* stance. Look right and pull back the left fist to the side. The right arm is placed horizontally in front of the solar plexus with the palm facing downwards.

Perform right *Chudan Mae-geri* to the right. At the same time, perform right *Yoko-barai* block at the height of the nose.

Step with left foot to the left and make left *Zenkutsu-dachi* stance. At the same time, perform *Gedan Kosa-uke* (cross-arm block) starting directly from the previous position. The right arm is on top of the left and both backs of the hands face forward.

Step forward with the right foot and make right *Nekoashi-dachi* stance. At the same time, perform right *Chudan Yoko-uke* block. The left arm is placed horizontally in front of the solar plexus with the palm facing upwards.

Move the left foot next to the right and make *Heisoku-dachi* stance. Look left and pull back the right fist to the side. The left arm is placed horizontally in front of the solar plexus with the palm facing downwards.

Perform left *Chudan Mae-geri* to the left. At the same time, perform left *Yoko-barai* block at the height of the nose.

Land forward and make right *Zenkutsu-dachi* stance. At the same time, open the right hand and bring it in front of the body and strike it with left *Hiji-ate* (elbow strike).

Turn the body to the left and shift stance to left *Sokkutsu-dachi*. At the same time, perform right *Sukui-uke* (scooping block) at shoulder height. The left hand should be placed in front of the forehead with the palm facing forward.

Keeping the upper body as it is, perform right *Chudan Mae-geri*.

Land forward and block downward with the left arm with closed fist. The right fist should be pulled back to the left shoulder.

Cross the left foot behind the right and make *Kosa-dachi* stance. At the same time, perform right *Jodan Ura-uchi* (back fist strike). The left fist is pulled back to the side.

Turn anti-clockwise on both feet through 225 degrees to face the left 45 degree line and make left *Nekoashi-dachi* stance. At the same time, perform left *Chudan Yoko-uke* block. The right fist is pulled back to the side.

Perform right *Chudan Mae-geri*.

Land forward and make right *Moto-dachi* stance. At the same time, perform right *Chudan Oi-zuki*. The left fist is pulled back to the side.

Follow up with right *Chudan Gyaku-zuki*.

Move the left foot and turn anti-clockwise through 45 degrees to face the rear. Make left *Nekoashi-dachi* stance and, at the same time, perform left *Chudan Yoko-uke* block. The right arm is placed horizontally in front of the solar plexus with the palm facing upwards.

(side view)

Step forward with the right foot and make right *Nekoashi-dachi* stance. At the same time, perform right *Chudan Yoko-uke* block. The right arm is crossed under the left before blocking. The left arm is placed horizontally in front of the solar plexus with the palm facing upwards.

Follow up with left *Chudan Gyaku-zuki*.

Move the right foot and turn clockwise through 90 degrees to face the right 45 degree line. Make right *Nekoashi-dachi* stance and, at the same time, perform right *Chudan Yoko-uke* block. The left fist is pulled back to the side.

Perform left *Chudan Mae-geri*.

Land forward and make left *Moto-dachi* stance. At the same time, perform left *Chudan Oi-zuki*. The right fist is pulled back to the side.

(side view)

Step forward with the left foot and make left *Nekoashi-dachi* stance. At the same time, perform left *Chudan Yoko-uke* block. The left arm is crossed under the right before blocking. The right arm is placed horizontally in front of the solar plexus with the palm facing upwards.

(side view)

Keeping the same stance, extend both arms forward at slightly higher than shoulder height with the palms facing towards yourself.

(side view)

Turn and close both hands in a grabbing action and pull them down to the sides of the body. At the same time, shift weight to the left leg and perform right *Hiza-geri* (knee kick).

(side view)

Move the right foot and make *Musubi-dachi* stance and bring hands to the sides of the thighs.

End of the Kata

Cross the right foot forward and left as you land, and turn anti-clockwise on both feet through 225 degrees to face the left 45 degree line. Make left *Nekoashi-dachi* stance and, at the same time, perform left *Chudan Shuto-uke* block. The right hand is placed in front of the solar plexus with the palm facing upwards.

Step right foot towards right 45 degree line, then the left foot follows the right to make right *Nekoashi-dachi* stance (*Yoriashi* – slide in). At the same time, perform right *Chudan Shuto-uke* block. The left hand is placed in front of the solar plexus with the palm facing upwards.

Slide back by moving the left foot back first, then the right, and make *Hachiji-dachi* (*Soto Hachiji-dachi*) stance facing the front. Both fists are placed in front of the thighs. Keep looking towards the last opponent at the right 45 degree direction for a period of one breath (*Zanshin*), then look forward.

Heian Godan

Musubi-dachi

Open the right foot to the right and make *Hachiji-dachi* (or *Soto-hachiji-dachi*) stance. Both fists are placed in front of thighs.

Pivot on the right foot and turn to the left. Move the left foot a little and make left *Nekoashi-dachi* stance. At the same time, perform left *Chudan Yoko-uke* block. The right fist is pulled back to the side.

Perform right *Chudan Gyaku-zuki*. The left fist is pulled back to the side.

Step forward with the right foot and make right *Zenkutsu-dachi* stance. At the same time, perform right *Chudan Yoko-uke* block. The left arm is placed horizontally in front of the solar plexus with the palm facing upwards.

Step forward with the left foot and make left *Zenkutsu-dachi* stance. At the same time, perform *Gedan Kosa-uke* block (cross-arm block) starting directly from the previous position. The right arm is on top of the left and the backs of both hands face forward.

Open both hands and lift them to make *Jodan Kosa-uke* block.

While moving the right foot slightly forward, roll both hands down so that the palm heels touch together.

Bring the left foot back and turn clockwise through 90 degrees to face the front. Pull the right fist to the side and place the left arm horizontally in front of the chest with the palm facing downwards (left *Chudan Kagi-zuki*).

Move the right foot and turn to the right to make right *Nekoashi-dachi* stance. At the same time, perform right *Chudan Yoko-uke* block. The left fist is pulled back to the side.

Perform left *Chudan Gyaku-zuki*. The right fist is pulled back to the side.

Bring the right foot back and turn anti-clockwise through 90 degrees to face the front. Pull the left fist to the side and place the right arm horizontally in front of the chest with the palm facing downwards (right *Chudan Kagi-zuki*).

Continue moving the right foot and make left side facing *Hachiji-dachi* (*Soto Hachiji-dachi*) stance. At the same time, perform left *Yoko-barai* block at shoulder height. The right fist is pulled back to the side.

(side view)

Step forward with the right foot and make right *Moto-dachi* stance. At the same time, perform right *Chudan Oi-zuki*. The left fist is pulled back to the side.

Turn anti-clockwise and step back with the right foot to make side facing *Shiko-dachi* stance. At the same time, perform right *Gedan Harai-uke* block. The left fist remains at the side.

(side view)

Move the left foot and turn anti-clockwise to face the front in left *Moto-dachi* stance. At the same time, perform left *Yoko-barai* block at shoulder height. The right fist is pulled back to the side.

Step forward with the right foot and, at the same time, strike the left palm with right *Hiji-ate* (elbow strike).

Step right foot to the right and make right *Zenkutsu-dachi* stance. At the same time, perform right *Chudan Yoko-uke* block. The left fist is placed inside the right elbow with palm facing upwards.

(side view)

Pivot both feet on the spot and make left *Kokutsu-dachi* stance. At the same time, cross the arms and perform left *Gedan Harai-uke* block. The right fist is pulled back at ear height.

Bring the left foot half way back.

138

Move the left foot and make right *Kosa-dachi* stance (crossed stance). At the same time, perform right *Chudan Yoko-uke* block. The left fist is placed under the right elbow with the palm facing downwards.

Move the left foot a little and look back. Stretch the left knee while keeping the left heel off the ground and lift both arms above the right shoulder.

(side view)

Step forward with the right foot and turn anti-clockwise through 90 degrees to face left while bringing the left foot behind the right to make right *Kosa-dachi* stance. At the same time, perform *Kosa-uke* block (cross block) with the right arm on top of the left.

Step in with the right foot and make right *Kokutsu-dachi* stance. At the same time, cross the arms and perform right *Gedan Hārai-uke* block. The left fist is pulled back to ear height.

Move back the right foot and make *Hachiji-dachi* (or *Soto-hachiji- dachi*) stance in *Shomen* position towards the front. Bring the fists in front of thighs. Keep looking towards the last opponent for a period of one breath (*Zanshin*), then look forward.

Move the right foot and make *Musubi-dachi* stance and bring hands to the sides of the thighs.

End of the Kata

法形組手

Pin'an Hokei Kumite

Introduction

'*Hokei*' means a set of pair works (*Kei*) to practise principles (*Ho*), and '*Hokei Kumite*' is a series of pre-arranged sparring techniques of which techniques are drawn from particular Katas. These five '*Pin'an Hokei Kumite*' are of course derived from *Pin'an* Katas.

Its origin or originator is not known, but I believe that '*Pin'an Hokei Kumite*' was created by Master Kenwa Mabuni and his senior students in mainland Japan as these are only practised in *Shito-ryu* based organizations. So, they are not practised only within *Tani-ha Shito-ryu*, but some other *Shito-ryu* organizations practise them as well. Of course some technical details are different between organizations but they are basically the same routines.

We learnt our version from Master Chojiro Tani, but modified some movements a little while keeping the original order so as to clarify the principles (*Riai*) and to follow the kata more closely.

The principles used in our '*Pin'an Hokei Kumite*' are as follows:

Nidan – Tenshin (change of angle or direction)

Shodan – Irimi (turning and entering of the body)

Sandan – Hanmi Nekoashi (quarter facing cat stance – turning and dropping of the body)

Yondan – Tenshin Irimi (simultaneous use of Tenshin and Irimi)

Godan – Kirikaeshi (sharp turning and turning back of the body)

Each '*Hokei Kumite*' consists of a series of attacks and defences, but they are never a long series – just 2 or 3 sets of attacks and counters. This conforms more to the ideals of '*Budo*' (Japanese Martial Arts).

The most important aspects of Martial Arts training are:

1 *Ki-Ken-Tai-no-Itchi* (unification of spirit, technique and body) and

2 *Sen* (initiative). (*refer to my book *Fundamentals of Karate-do*)

In order to practise a long series of pre-arranged sparring, one would have to subdue these two most important attitudes of Martial Arts. Such a practice could therefore have a negative effect.

On the other hand, these short sequences of '*Hokei Kumite*' actually encourage practitioners to put everything in a short burst, and mental attitude forms a very important aspect of the practice.

You should remember that all Karate techniques are potentially knock-out techniques : the intention behind techniques is that they should be powerful enough to knock out the opponent with every move. Otherwise, you cannot achieve the state of '*Ki-Ken-Tai-no-Itchi*' nor '*Sen*'. Therefore you must apply control to all techniques.

On the technical side, just to remember the sequences and keep repeating them is not good enough. You must understand the technical principles involved in every move and endeavour to use them each time you practise rather than just performing the basic movements. In this way, you will become familiar with these principles and will become able to use them in various other applications as appropriate.

In addition to the principles specific to *Pin'an Hokei Kumite* already mentioned above, other general principles you must pay attention to while practising are:

1 Five principles of blocking
  i *Rakka* (hard block)
  ii *Ryusui* (soft block)
  iii *Kusshin* (up and down movements of the body)
  iv *Ten'i* (change position and angle of the body) – (Although this is very similar to the *Tenshin* principle mentioned above, *Tenshin* is more specifically used for 'change of direction' whereas *Ten'i* is more general.)
  v *Hangeki* (counter)
2 Three ways of producing shock
  i Dropping of the body
  ii Expansion and contraction of the body
  iii Fixation of all the muscles of the body
3 Internal changing weight

These three aspects of training are dealt with more thoroughly in my book *Fundamentals of Karate-do*.

To these I would like to add another very important principle which is:
Every time you move your body (your mass), in whatever way (forwards/backwards, up/down, etc.), it will create energy. As Karate techniques are aimed at producing maximum effect with minimum effort, all energy produced must be used and should not be wasted. This means that, every time

you move, the movement should directly connect to techniques. So, if you use *Kusshin* and *Ten'i* to defend yourself, your blocking techniques must be executed as you move. The same applies to attacking techniques as well.

You must remember that you are not fighting with your partner when practising these sets but helping each other to learn and practise. You have to synchronize with your partner concentrating on correct distance and timing as well as maintaining good stance and posture. Also, you should not alter the techniques, otherwise you will not be learning the principles involved.

Please remember to bow to your partner at the beginning and at the end of the practice.

Face each other in *Musubi-dachi* stance.

Rei (bow)

Yoi (open left foot then the right to make *Heiko-dachi* stance)

Kamae (on guard) in *Moto-dachi* stance

At the end, you have to reverse the order.

The following explanations are from left foot forward position (*Hidari-gamae*), but you should practise from right foot forward position (*Migi-gamae*) as well. To facilitate the explanation, **A** stands for 'Attacker' and **B** stands for 'Blocker'.

A Attack B with right *Chudan Mae-geri* (front kick).
B Step back with the left foot and block A's kick with right *Gedan Harai-uke*. – As A starts right *Mae-geri*, B starts to step back with the left foot to keep away, remembering to move the centre of gravity back. At the same time, B's right fist approaches the left shoulder, to prepare the block as well as to cover the body. This involves a slight contraction of the body as well. As the left foot completes the stepping back process to make right foot forward stance, B blocks A's kick with right *Gedan Harai-uke*. Principles involved in this movement are *Rakka*, *Kusshin* and *Ten'i*.

A Step forward with the left foot and attack with left *Jodan Oi-zuki*.
B As A starts to come forward, step back and across with the right foot.

B Move the left foot in and make *Moto-dachi* stance to counter with left *Jodan Maeken-zuki*. With this foot work (*Tenshin*), B avoids A's attack and counter attacks simultaneously. – Although the right foot moves before the left, both feet must move almost simultaneously and the body must turn quite sharply. The principles involved in this movement are *Ten'i* and *Hangeki*.

* After a period (about two breaths) of *Zanshin* (reserved mind), A moves back by two steps while B follows A and moves forward by two steps to return to the starting position.

A Land forward and attack with right *Jodan Oi-zuki*.
B Shift weight to the rear leg and make right *Nekoashi-dachi* (cat stance) and block A's punch with right *Uchi-otoshi* block. – You should remember to block as you change the stance, thus using the energy produced by changing stance directly on to the block. Do not block after changing the stance. Principles used in this movement are *Rakka*, *Kusshin* and *Ten'i*.

N o t e

When stepping back and blocking with *Gedan Harai-uke*, you should not open the right elbow as this photo shows. This action makes an opening as well as slowing down your blocking action.

Instead, you have to keep your right elbow well closed when stepping back to protect the body as explained above.

A Step forward with the right foot and attack with right *Jodan Oi-zuki*.

B Change stance to *Nekoashi-dachi* (cat stance) in *Hanmi* position and, at the same time, block A's attack with left *Jodan Yoko-uke* block. The right fist covers the forehead like in the *Pin'an Shodan* Kata. – The block must be performed as B changes stance thus using the drop of the body. This change of stance into *Nekoashi-dachi* brings the body further away from the attack as well as producing power by virtue of the dropping motion of the body. These two aspects are the great advantages of shifting stance into *Nekoashi-dachi*. Another advantage of *Nekoashi-dachi* is to free the front foot for counter-attacking. The principles used in this movement are *Rakka* and *Kusshin*.

B Slide forward and turn the body into *Ma-hanmi* position in *Heiko-dachi* stance. At the same time, strike A's temple with left *Kentsui-uchi* (hammer fist strike). – These actions of sliding-in, turning of the body and *Kentsui- uchi* attack must be performed simultaneously as one whole-body movement.

A Slide back and block B's strike with right *Shuto Yoko-uchi* block. – This block must be performed as A slides back using *Ten'i* principle. The nature of the block is *Rakka*.

A Push B's striking hand away with left *Shuto* (knife hand).

146

2

A Follow up with left *Chudan Gyaku-zuki* aimed at B's stomach just under his blocking arm's elbow.

B Remain in *Nekoashi-dachi* but move the left hip back to make *Shomen* position. As you turn the body to *Shomen* position, drop the left elbow to cover and protect the body. At the same time, block A's punch with right *Kentsui Uchi-otoshi* (strike-down block with hammer fist). – This movement involves slight contraction and dropping of the body as well. The nature of the block is *Rakka*.

5

A Attack with left *Mae-geri* kick.

B Step back with left foot and make right *Zenkutsu-dachi* stance and, at the same time, block A's kick with right *Gedan Harai-uke*. – When A pushes B's hand away, B senses A's intention and starts to step back.

Principles involved in this movement are the same as the first movement of '*Hokei Kumite Pin'an Nidan*'.

Continued next page

6

A Land forward and attack with right *Jodan Gyaku-zuki*.
B Move the right foot forward a little and turn the body
into *Ma-hanmi* position. Lean slightly forward to make *Irimi*
position. Left foot should be turned anti-clockwise and
moved slightly to the right to follow the movement of the
body to facilitate the action. At the same time, perform left
Jodan Age-uke block and right *Chudan Ura-zuki* punch
simultaneously. – The turning of the body and slight shifting
of the weight forward involved in moving into *Irimi*
position is used to produce the power of both block and
attack, as well as avoiding A's attack. Thus all these
movements must be performed simultaneously. Also, the
fist of left *Jodan Age-uke* block must point towards A's face
so that it can become an attack if A comes forward too
closely. The principles involved in this movement are *Ten'i*,
Rakka and *Hangeki*.

* After a period of *Zanshin*, A moves back by two steps
while B follows A and moves forward by one step to
return to the starting position.

Turning of the body is one of the most important factors in *Pin'an Hokei Kumite Shodan*.

Shomen position in *Moto-dachi* stance.

Hanmi position in *Nekoashi-dachi* stance.

Shomen position in *Nekoashi-dachi* stance.

Ma-hanmi position in *Heiko-dachi* stance.

Shomen position in *Zenkutsu-dachi* stance.

Ma-hanmi position in *Zenkutsu-dachi* stance. (*Irimi* position)

A Step forward with right foot and attack B with right *Chudan Oi-zuki*.

B Step back with left foot and block A's punch with right *Ninoude-uke* (bent-arm inward block). – Stepping back and the block must be coordinated to use the body movement to produce the power of the block. The principles used are *Ten'i* and *Rakka*.

B Slide forward and counter-attack A's body with right punch (*Chudan-zuki*). – Like the block, the body movement of sliding-in must be coordinated with the punch.

A Slide back and block B's punch with right *Uchi Harai-uke* (or *Uchibarai*, straight arm inward sweeping block) which should be performed directly from the punching position and coordinated with the slide-back. The principles used in this movement are *Ten'i* and *Ryusui*, so the block must re-direct the punch rather than parry it hard.

A Step forward with left foot and attack with left *Chudan Oi-zuki*.

B Move right foot back then left foot slightly forward, and make left *Nekoashi-dachi* stance in *Hanmi* position. This action involves sharp turning and dropping of the body. At the same time, perform right *Gedan Harai-uke* and left *Jodan Ura-uchi* simultaneously. – When B steps back, he should go back less than the advance of A. So, in a way, B lets A approach, then intercepts A's attack with *Harai-uke* as he suddenly drops his body into *Nekoashi-dachi* stance with simultaneous attack. The principles used here are *Ten'i*, *Kusshin* and *Rakka*. The *Nekoashi-dachi* A drops into is in *Hanmi* position, which involves an extra 45 degree turn of the body. This turn of the body effectively changes the direction of *Harai-uke* block so as to re-direct A's punch. Thus this block is a hard *Rakka* block, but contains a certain amount of *Ryusui* element.

* After a period of *Zanshin*, A moves back by two steps while B follows A and moves forward by two steps to return to the starting position.

N o t e

Although B blocks with *Ninoude-uke* in *Moto-dachi* stance in the explanation above, B can do it in *Shiko-dachi* stance like in the Kata. In this case, B should slide forward and attack A in *Shiko-dachi* stance as well.

Yondan

A Step forward with right foot and attack B with right *Jodan Oi-zuki*.
B Slide back and block A's punch with left *Jodan Sukui-uke* (scooping block). – The block and slide-back must be coordinated to produce the power of the block. The principles used are *Ten'i* and *Ryusui*. Although *Sukui-uke* is supposed to be a soft block, it can still produce a certain amount of impact. So it contains some *Rakka* aspect as well.

B Slide forward and attack A with right *Chudan Gyaku-zuki*.
A Slide back and block the punch with right *Shotei Osae-uke* (pressing down block with palm heel). – Like B's previous blocking movement, the slide back must be coordinated with the block to produce power. The principles used here are *Ten'i* and *Rakka*.

B Move left foot to the right and turn it anti-clockwise so that you can get into *Irimi* position at a diagonal angle (*Tenshin*). At the same time, attack A's neck with right *Shuto-uchi* (knife hand strike). Left open hand is placed in front of the solar plexus with palm facing upwards.
*After a period of *Zanshin*, A moves back by two steps while B follows A and moves forward by one step to return to the starting position.

Note

Although B's last technique is called *Shuto-uchi* (knife hand strike), it is a cutting action rather than a striking action. When B moves the rear foot and strikes, his body turns more than usual (into *Ma-hanmi* position) and leans slightly forward thus making *Irimi* position. This move is typical of cutting with a Japanese sword. As with the sword, B can use *Oshigiri* (push cut) action or *Hikigiri* (pull cut) action when striking with *Shuto*. When using *Oshigiri* (push cut) action, the *Shuto* must be pushed through the neck as though squashing the carotid artery. When using *Hikigiri* (pull cut) action, the *Shuto* must hook behind the neck. Both modes of action can also be used to break the collar bone. These strikes are potentially quite dangerous, so extreme care must be taken when practising.

A Step forward with left foot and attack with left *Jodan Oi-zuki*.

B Step back with left foot and block A's punch with right *Haishu Nagashi-uke* (let-go block with back of hand). This block is performed by inserting and pulling back the blocking hand between the oncoming punch and its target (the face) to direct it away to the side. It is not a hard striking block : ideally no impact is felt by the attacker. Left hand is positioned inside right elbow. – As usual, the body movement of stepping back must be coordinated with the block. The principles used are *Ten'i* and *Ryusui*.

B Step right foot to the right and push A's arm to the right to open up the target area (neck).

pull-cut

push-cut

153

Godan

1

A Step forward with right foot and attack with right *Jodan Oi-zuki.*
B Slide back and block with *Kaisho Jodan Kosa-uke* (cross block with open hands). – The block and slide-back must be coordinated. The principle used here is *Ten'i*, while *Jodan Kosa-uke* can be performed hard according to *Rakka* principle as well as performed softly to re-direct the punch using *Ryusui* principle.

2

A Follow up with left *Chudan Gyaku-zuki.*
B Roll down both hands and block with right wrist supported by left palm heel (*Awase-Osae-uke*, press-down block with two hands together). – The principle used here is *Rakka*.

5

A Land forward and attack with left *Jodan Oi-zuki.*
B Move the right foot back and turn back the body sharply to make right *Nekoashi-dachi* stance in *Hanmi* position. At the same time, block the punch with right *Chudan Yoko-uke.* Although A's punch was aimed to the face in *Kokutsu-dachi* stance, as *Nekoashi-dachi* is higher than *Kokutsu-dachi*, *Yoko-uke* block ends up at *Chudan* height.
– The principles used are *Ten'i*, *Kusshin* and *Rakka.*

6

B Slide in from right heel, attack A with left *Chudan Gyaku-zuki* in right *Nekoashi-dachi* stance. Keep *Yoko-uke* block in place as you slide in to punch, so that the slide-in action will put the opponent off balance.
* After a period of *Zanshin*, A moves back by two steps while B follows A and moves forward by one step to return to the starting position.

B Slide forward and turn the body into *Ma-hanmi* position in *Heiko-dachi* stance. At the same time, attack A with left *Jodan Kentsui-uchi* (hammer fist strike).
A Slide back and block with right *Jodan Shuto Yoko-uchi* block. – The principles used are *Ten'i* and *Rakka*.

A Attack with left *Mae-geri*.
B Step back with left foot and turn the body sharply into *Kokutsu-dachi* stance. At the same time, block the kick with right *Gedan Harai-uke*. – The principles used are *Ten'i*, *Kusshin* and *Rakka*.

Note

When B steps back with hip width stance then turns into *Kokutsu-dachi*, B automatically puts himself into a slightly angled position (*Tenshin*).

Pin'an Kumite

Introduction

Although *Pin'an Hokei Kumite* was derived from Pin'an Katas and provides a good basis for practising the principles involved, it does not cover the whole spectrum of techniques in these Katas. So, we created extra sets called 'Pin'an Kumite' in order to practise techniques which are not covered in *Pin'an Hokei Kumite*.

If you practise both *Pin'an Hokei Kumite* and *Pin'an Kumite*, you will be covering most of the important techniques from *Pin'an* Katas thus your understanding of these Katas will be more complete.

Again, please remember that you are not competing or fighting with your partner but helping each other to improve techniques and understanding. You have to synchronize with your partner using correct distance and timing as well as maintaining good stance and posture.

Tenshin (change of angle or direction) principle is used extensively throughout these sets.

Of course, you should not forget 'the five principles of blocking' either.

1 *Rakka* (hard block)

2 *Ryusui* (soft block)

3 *Kusshin* (up and down movements of the body)

4 *Ten'i* (change position and angle of the body). (Although this is very similar to *Tenshin* principle mentioned above, *Tenshin* is more specifically used for 'change of direction' whereas *Ten'i* is more general.)

5 *Hangeki* (counter)

Also, all aspects I explained for *Pin'an Hokei Kumite* apply to *Pin'an Kumite* as well.

Please also remember to bow to your partner at the beginning and at the end of the practice.

1. Face each other in *Musubi-dachi* stance.

2. *Rei* (bow)

3. *Yoi* (open left foot then the right to make *Heiko-dachi* stance)

4. *Kamae* (on guard) in *Moto-dachi* stance

At the end, you have to reverse the order.

The following explanations are from left foot forward position (*Hidari-gamae*), but you should practise from right foot forward position (*Migi-gamae*) as well. To facilitate the explanation, **A** stands for 'Attacker' and **B** stands for 'Blocker'.

Nidan

A Slide in and attack with left *Jodan Maeken-zuki* (leading hand punch).
B Side step to the right (move right foot first then the left) and change angle a little (*Tenshin*) to keep facing A. At the same time, block A's punch with left *Jodan Age-uke*. – Jodan block and side-step must be executed simultaneously as one whole body movement. The principles used are *Ten'i* and *Rakka*.

B Slide in and counter attack with right *Chudan Gyaku-zuki*.
A Side step to the right and change angle (*Tenshin*) to keep facing B. At the same time, block B's punch with left *Gedan Harai-uke*. – Like B's previous movement, Gedan block and side-step must be executed simultaneously as one whole body movement. The principles used are *Ten'i* and *Rakka*.

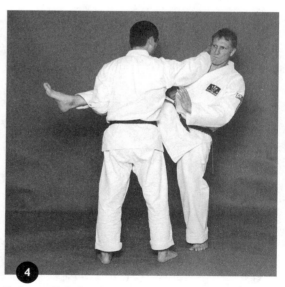

A Attack with right *Chudan Mae-geri*.
B Avoid the kick by moving left foot forward and to the right and turn the body into *Ma-hanmi* position in *Shiko-dachi* stance. At the same time, block with left *Shuto-barai*. – The principles used are *Ten'i* and *Kusshin*. The block can be performed either in *Rakka* (hard) or *Ryusui* (soft) manner.

B Scoop A's kicking leg with left arm and step forward with right foot to attack A's neck with right *Shuto-uchi*.

5 **B** Move left foot next to the right.

6 **B** Pivoting on left foot, turn clockwise and step right foot back. At the same time, catch the back of A's head with right hand.

9 **B** Press A's head down against the ground with left hand. Do not press too hard or too quickly as it will result in A's head banging on the floor.

10 **B** Punch A's neck with right fist.

* After A stands up, both should go back to the starting position.

7

B Keep on turning and throw A down by lifting his leg and lowering his head forward.

8

B Turn A's head clockwise using both hands. Be careful not to turn the head too quickly as it might damage A's neck.

Note

A must be thrown forward and not backwards. If A is thrown backwards, B will lose control and will not be able to finish off properly.

Shodan

A Slide in and attack with left *Chudan Maeken-zuki*.
B Side step to the right and change stance into left *Nekoashi-dachi* and turn a little to keep facing A (*Tenshin*). At the same time, block A's punch with left *Chudan Shuto-uke* (knife hand block). – The principles used are *Ten'i*, *Kusshin* and *Rakka*.

A Slide in from left foot towards B, attack with right *Chudan Gyaku-zuki*.
B Slide to the left and turn the body into *Gyaku-hanmi* position to avoid the punch. Right knee should be turned in to close the groin. At the same time, block with right *Chudan Yoko-uke*. – The principles used are *Ten'i* and *Rakka*.

B Catch A's upper arm and pull him forward.

B Strike A's neck with right forearm with *Jodan Age-uke*-like movement.

*A slides back and B steps back to go back to the starting position.

B Counter attack with right *Chudan Mae-geri.*

B Land forward and follow up with left *Chudan Gyaku-zuki.*

Note

When going into *Gyaku-hanmi* position, B must make sure to close his groin to prevent possible attack by A (see pictures right).

When attacking A's neck, B should not move forward. Instead, B must pull A so that A falls forward off balance onto B's strike.

wrong position with groin open

correct position with groin closed

A Approaching from behind, wrap B's body and arms with both arms.
B As A approaches and wraps both arms around you, open both elbows to create resistance.

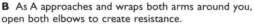

B Slide and turn the body towards the left to upset A's balance forward.

B Step right foot forward and lean forward to pull A forward and stretch his arms.

B Cross left foot and turn anti-clockwise. At the same time, hit A's arms up and across using left elbow and forearm. Pull right fist back to disengage A's grip.

B Turn back the body and strike A's body with right *Ushiro Hiji-ate* (elbow strike towards rear) and punch A's face with left fist over the right shoulder.

A Catch B's right wrist with both hands and twist it up his back.

B *Chudan Gyaku-zuki.*

* A steps back and A and B face each other to finish.

A Slide in and attack with left *Jodan Maeken-zuki*.
B Side step to the right and change angle a little to keep facing A (*Tenshin*). At the same time, lift left arm and block A's punch with left *Haishu-uke* (back of hand block). – Block and side-step must be executed simultaneously as one whole body movement. The principle used is *Ten'i*. The block can be performed either in *Rakka* (hard) or *Ryusui* (soft) manner.

A Slide in from left foot towards B and attack with right *Jodan Gyaku-zuki*.
B Move right foot back and turn left foot and body clockwise to make left *Kokutsu-dachi* (back stance). At the same time, block A's punch with left *Jodan Yoko-barai* (side sweeping block). – You must block as you turn the body. The principles used are *Ten'i* and *Rakka*.

B Scrape A's neck with right forearm while lifting right hand.

B Catch the back of A's neck and pull him forward. At the same time, kick his stomach with right *Hiza-geri* (knee kick).

3

B Catch A's punching arm with left hand and counter attack with left *Chudan Yoko-geri* (side kick).

4

B Land forward and turn the body anti-clockwise to face A. At the same time, strike A's body with Mawashi *Hiji-ate* (roundhouse elbow strike). – Landing of the foot, turning of the body and striking with elbow must be done simultaneously as one whole body movement.

7

B Push A away and land back to face each other in *Moto-dachi* stance in readiness for Part 2.

A Slide in and attack with left *Jodan Maeken-zuki*.
B Side step to the right and change angle a little to keep facing A (*Tenshin*). At the same time, block A's punch with left *Jodan Yoko-uke*. – Side-step and block must be executed simultaneously as one whole body movement. The principles involved are *Ten'i* and *Rakka*.

A Slide in from left foot towards B, attack with right *Chudan Gyaku-zuki*.
B Block with *Gedan Harai-uke*. – The principle involved is *Rakka*.

A Land forward and follow up with right *Jodan Oi-zuki*.
B Move left foot back and turn body anti-clockwise to face A in *Moto-dachi* stance. At the same time, block A's punch upwards with left palm. – The principles involved are *Kusshin* and *Ryusui*.

B Using left wrist, turn A's punching arm anti-clockwise so that the elbow points downwards. At the same time, push A's right elbow up with right palm.

3

B Counter attack with right *Chudan Gyaku-zuki*.
A Change stance into left *Nekoashi-dachi* and block B's punch with left *Chudan Yoko-uke* as you change stance. – The principles involved are *Kusshin* and *Rakka*.

4

A Move left foot back a little to adjust the distance and attack with right *Mae-geri*.
B Move right foot back and turn left foot and body clockwise to make left *Kokutsu-dachi* stance. At the same time, block A's kick with left *Shotei Harai-uke* (sweeping block with palm) while right palm covers the forehead. – You should block as you turn the body and change stance. The principles involved are *Ten'i*, *Kusshin* and *Rakka*.

7

B Kick A's stomach with right *Mae-geri*.

8

B Land forward and cross left foot in to make right *Kosa-dachi* stance. At the same time, strike A's face with right *Jodan Ura-uchi* (back fist strike). – You should strike as you cross the left foot so that the whole body is behind the strike.

B Catch A's right shoulder with right hand and move the left foot back.

B Turn the body anti-clockwise, shift weight onto left leg and stretch right leg

B Drop right knee onto A's hind rib and push his right elbow against left knee using left hand.

B Finish off with right *Tsuki* onto A's rib.

* After A stands up, both should go back to the starting position.

to throw A with *Tai-otoshi* (body drop throw).

B Still holding A's wrist with left hand, push his right elbow with right hand and turn him half way onto his stomach.

Note

1 *Haishu-uke* should be performed in an upward and outward manner, and not just outward.

2 Although I explained to push A's right elbow up with right palm, you actually should use the edge of index finger and palm to be more effective.

A Attack with right *Chudan Mae-geri*.
B Move the right foot back a little, shift stance to left *Kokutsu-dachi* and block A's kick with left *Gedan Harai-uke*.

A Land forward and attack with right *Jodan Oi-zuki*
B Move back the left foot a little and turn back the body to face A in left *Moto-dachi* stance. At the same time, block A's punch with left *Jodan Yoko-barai*.

B Push A's chest with left shoulder.

B Step in with left foot and make *Heiko-dachi* stance in *Ma-hanmi* position. At the same time, attack A's temple with left *Kentsui-uchi* (hammer fist strike).
A Step back with left foot and make right *Moto-dachi* stance. Block the strike with right *Jodan Yoko-uchi* as you step back. – The principles involved are *Ten'i* and *Rakka*.

3

A Attack with left *Mae-geri*.
B Move left foot back and slightly to the left then move right foot forward to make right forward *Shiko-dachi* stance at an angle. At the same time, block the kick with right *Gedan Harai-uke*. – You must block as you drop into *Shiko-dachi* stance. The principles involved are *Ten'i*, *Kusshin* and *Rakka*.

4

B Counter attack with left *Chudan Kagi-zuki* (hook punch).
A Land forward and block the punch with left *Gedan Harai-uke*. – The principle involved is *Rakka*.

7

A Push B's striking arm with left *Shuto* (knife hand).

8

A Left *Chudan Mae-geri*.
B Slide back and make left *Moto-dachi* stance. At the same time, block the kick with left *Gedan Harai-uke*. Simultaneously, hit A's shin with right *Tsuki*. – The principles involved are *Ten'i*, *Kusshin*, *Rakka* and *Hangeki*.

A Land forward and attack with right *Jodan Gyaku-zuki*.
B Block the punch with *Jodan Kosa-uke*. – This block can be executed with *Rakka* (hard) or *Ryusui* (soft) principle.

B Roll down the hands and catch A's wrist while pressing down his right elbow with left elbow. Step left foot forward into *Shiko-dachi* stance to give added pressure to the joint.

B Strike A's head with left *Kentsui-uchi*.

* A moves back two steps and both return to starting position.

分解組手

Pin'an Bunkai Kumite

Introduction

As I explained earlier, *Pin'an Hokei Kumite* and *Pin'an Kumite* together cover most of the techniques contained in *Pin'an* Katas. So, by practising them regularly, your understanding of *Pin'an* Katas will be greatly enhanced.

On the other hand, although its main weapons are punching, kicking and striking together with blocking, Karate is an all round self defence system containing many throwing and joint attacking techniques as well.

When we analyse techniques in Kata and their applications, we have to consider several different possibilities. It is not the case that there is only one meaning for a movement or technique in a kata. A seemingly obvious simple punch may also be used for blocking, disengaging or throwing. In the same sense, a seemingly obvious simple block may also be used for attacking, disengaging, throwing or joint breaking.

These sets of *Pin'an Bunkai Kumite* were created to show practitioners applications other than the rather straight forward applications practised in *Pin'an Hokei Kumite* and *Pin'an Kumite*. Each set is composed of 1) initial block, 2) counter attack, 3) take down, 4) immobilisation and 5) finishing off. 'Initial block' and 'counter attack' are direct applications of techniques or movements from Kata, but what happens afterwards is not covered in the Kata. This second part is called 'further application' (*Ohyoh* in Japanese). This approach is the traditional way of practising and studying Katas. The sets have been designed to a) incorporate a variety of principles and advanced techniques and b) avoid repetition of the same techniques. If a practitioner practises these sets regularly rather than choosing applications at random , he or she will then be reinforcing essential elements of the art of karate-do.

Also, I have defined which vital point to strike with each attacking technique in *Pin'an Bunkai Kumite*. In recent years I think many people have developed an interest in vital points (hitting points and pressure points) whereas

in the past I think they were more interested in developing a strong body and increasing their hitting power. It is said that the human body has 365 vital points. In that case, if you hit an opponent hard anywhere on his body, you are bound to hit some vital points! Anyway, knowledge of vital points (*Kyusho* in Japanese) has been an important part of any oriental martial arts school. Although there are very sophisticated vital points systems based on Chinese traditional medicine, what happened usually was that each of those schools chose a number of the more effective vital points out of so many to be incorporated into its own system. As the number of those more effective points is fairly limited, a kind of consensus was soon established. The points and their names mentioned in this chapter are widely used in many Japanese martial arts schools.

In case you want to find out exactly where these vital points are, I have given the number and the name of the meridian for each point so that you can refer to a good acupuncture book.

To facilitate the explanation, **A** stands for 'Attacker' and **B** stands for 'Blocker'. Remember to practise the sets on the opposite side of the body as well.

At the start of each set A and B face each other in a relaxed, natural position.

Ipponme (No. I) Tsukiage from *Pin'an Shodan* (Tsukiage = punch upwards)

A Step right foot, then left foot, forward, left *Jodan Oi-zuki*. Or step left foot forward then slide in, left *Jodan Maeken-zuki*.

B Advance the left foot diagonally towards the left, followed by the right foot to make left *Nekoashi-dachi* stance. At the same time, block A's punch with right *Age-uke* and strike the chin with left *Age-zuki*.

B Catch A's left wrist with the right hand and twist it down.

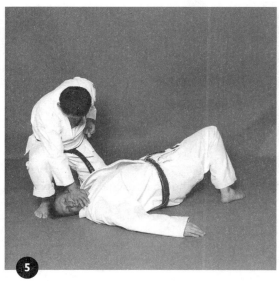

B Push the opponent's chin, thus twisting the neck, with the right hand. Drop the left knee on A's left upper-arm. (As this can cause intense pain, in practice place the knee on the forearm.)

B Strike A's neck (*Murasame*, left LI-17) with left *Nakataka-Ippon-Ken*.

B Strike the neck with left *Kentsui-uchi*.

B Slide the left hand down along A's left arm and catch A's left wrist. Hold the back of A's collar from behind with the right hand. Kick the back of A's left knee (*Shikkoku*, BL-54) with the sole of the right foot and pull him down on his back.

Nihonme (No. 2) Gyakuhanmi from *Pin'an Shodan* (Gyakuhanmi = reverse *Hanmi* position)

A Step left foot forward then *Yoriashi* (slide-in), right *Chudan Gyaku-zuki*.

B Advance left foot diagonally towards left and block A's punch with left *Shotei Yoko-uchi* block. This is a preliminary block.

B Advance right foot diagonally towards left as well and turn the body into *Gyaku-hanmi* position closing right knee to protect the groin. At the same time, block A's punch with right *Yoko-uke* block. This is the main block.

B Slide the left hand down A's upper arm to a natural stopping point just above the elbow (*Soto-hijizume*, TH-10 and *Uchi-hijizume*, HC-3) and squeeze his throat (*Koka*, ST-10) with the right hand.

B Turn A to the left and kick the back of his right knee (*Shikkoku*, BL-54) with left sole. Push him down to the ground on his back.

B Kick inside of A's left knee (*Kekkai*, SP-10) with right *Kakato-geri* (heel kick).

B Land forward and left *Gyaku-zuki* to A's rib (*Inazuma*, right SP-16/SP-21, the left side is called *Denko*) with *Nakataka-Ippon-Ken*.

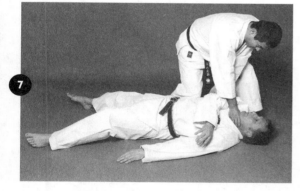

B Drop the right knee on the side of A's lower stomach (*Myoken*, SP-14).

B Drop right elbow to control A's right elbow.

B Strike the bridge of A's nose (*Sankon/Biko*) with left *Ura-uchi*.

Sanbonme (No. 3) Uchiage from *Pin'an Shodan* and *Nidan*

(Uchiage = strike upwards)

A Step left foot, then right foot forward, right *Chudan Oi-zuki*.

B Step left foot to the left, then right foot forward to make right *Moto-dachi* stance. At the same time, block A's punch with right *Gedan Harai-uke*.

B Catch A's right wrist with right hand and hit A's upper arm with left *Yoko-uchi*.

B Push A's right knee with left knee and pull him down backwards.

B Drop left knee on his temple (*Kasumi*, GB-5 and *Ryomo*, GB-3), press A's right arm against right knee to lock the elbow.

B Step left foot forward and strike A's neck (*Matsukaze*, right LI-17) with left forearm.

B Push A's chin with left forearm and push chest forward to lock A's right elbow.

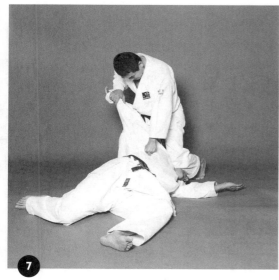

B Punch A's rib (*Inazuma*, right SP-16/SP-21) with left *Nakataka-Ippon-Ken*.

Yonhonme (No. 4) **Uchiotoshi** from *Pin'an Nidan*

(Uchiotoshi = strike downwards)

A Step left foot, then right foot forward and grab B's left wrist with right hand.

B Grab A's right wrist with right hand, step right foot back and make left *Nekoashi-dachi* stance. At the same time, pull and twist left hand to disengage.

B Step through with the left foot and push A to the ground.

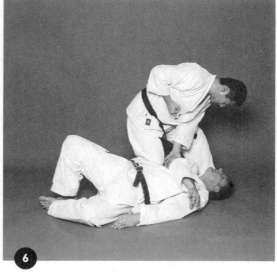

B Drop right knee to A's floating rib (*Getsuei*, LV-14) and press his right arm across the chest with left hand.

B Pull A forward with right hand and strike his temple (*Kasumi*, GB-5) with left *Kentsui-uchi*.

B Slide down left hand and grab A's upper arm just above the elbow (*Soto-hijizume*, TH-10 & *Uchi-hijizume*, HC-3). Step right foot forward behind A's right foot and strike his chin upwards with *Shotei-uchi*.

B Punch to the throat (*Kochu*) with right *Nakataka-Ippon-Ken*.

Gohonme (No. 5) Mawashi-nage · from *Pin'an Shodan & Nidan*
(Mawashi-nage = round throw)

A Step left foot, then right foot forward, right *Chudan Oi-zuki.*
B Step right foot back and block A's punch with left *Gedan Harai-uke.*

B Step right foot forward, push A's right knee from inside with own right knee and strike the neck (*Matsukaze*, right LI-17) with right forearm (*Jodan Age-uke* movement).

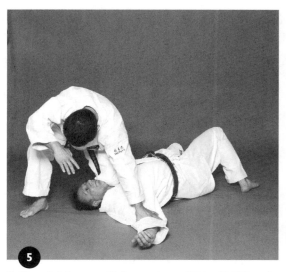

B Drop left knee on his lower throat (*Hichu*, CV-22) and press his right arm against the floor with left hand.

B Strike between his eyebrows (*Miken*) with right *Shotei-uchi.*

188

B Press A's head down from behind with right hand, step left foot forward, lift his left arm backwards with left hand and turn him round.

B Step right foot to the right and bring A to the ground on his back.

Ropponme (No. 6) Ryo-uke *from Pin'an Sandan*

(Ryo-uke = double block)

A Step right foot forward, then slide in, left *Chudan Gyaku-zuki*.
B Step right foot diagonally forward and to the right, then left foot diagonally backwards and to the right, and make right *Moto-dachi* stance at a slight angle (*Tenshin*). At the same time, block A's punch with left *Gedan Harai-uke* and strike his face (*Jinchu*, GV-26) with *Ura-uchi* simultaneously.

B Grab A's left wrist with left hand, press left upper arm with right hand just above the elbow joint, locking his elbow joint as well as putting him off balance.

B Drop right knee on his hind floating rib (*Ushiro-Denko*, BL-44, right side is called *Ushiro-Inazuma*). Give pressure to his left shoulder by pressing his left arm with left knee, simultaneously pressing his left shoulder down with right hand. Then, left *Tsuki* to between shoulder blades (*Sakkatsu*, GV-11) with *Seiken*.

B Step right foot forward.

B Then step left foot forward and press A down to the ground on his stomach.

Nanahonme (No. 7) Uchikomi from *Pin'an Yondan*

(Uchikomi = strike in)

1

A Step right foot, then left foot forward, left *Jodan Oi-zuki*. Or step left foot forward then slide in, left *Jodan Maeken-zuki*.
B Advance the left foot diagonally towards left, then right foot and make left *Nekoashi-dachi*. At the same time, block A's punch with right open hand *Age-uke*. Simultaneously, strike the neck (*Murasame*, left LI-17) with left *Shuto-uchi*.

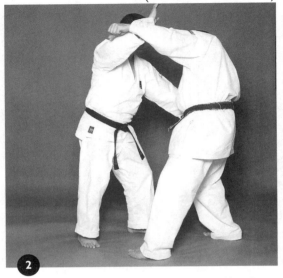

2

B Sliding left hand across A's upper body, grab A's right upper arm with left hand and pull down to upset his balance.

5

B Hold behind the neck with right hand and pull down. At the same time, kick solar plexus (*Suigetsu*, CV-14) with right *Hiza-geri*.

6

B Approaching from inside, wrap his right arm with left arm.

192

B Slide right hand along the inside of A's left arm and strike collar bone (*Erishita*, ST-12) with *Shuto-uchi*.

B Push and slide right arm against the right side of A's neck.

B Push A down to the floor on his stomach and drop left knee on his kidney (*Ushiro-Getsuei*, GB-25). Push the body forward and give pressure to his shoulder joint.

B Strike the back of neck (*Keichu*, GV-15) with *Shuto-uchi*.

Hachihonme (No. 8) Hikiotoshi from *Pin'an Godan*
(Hikiotoshi = pull down)

1

A Step left foot, then right foot forward, right *Chudan Oi-zuki*.

B Move right foot to the right a little, then step left foot forward and make left *Nekoashi-dachi* stance. At the same time, block A's punch with left *Chudan Yoko-uke*.

2

B Slide in a little and attack solar plexus (*Suigetsu*, CV-14) with right *Chudan Gyaku-zuki*.

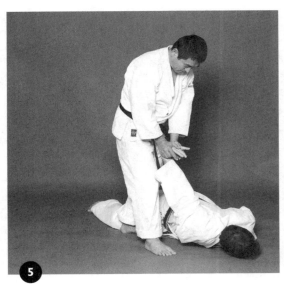

5

B Step right foot forward and push both hands down to bring A to the floor on his stomach.

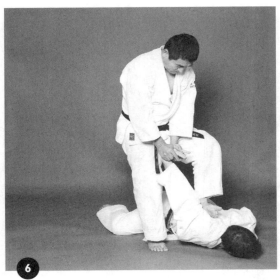

6

B Kick A's right shoulder with the outer edge of left foot (*Sokuto*).

B Hold A's right fist with right hand first.

B Then, with both hands. Step left foot diagonally forward towards left, then follow with right foot and turn the body clockwise into *Ma-hanmi* position. At the same time, pull both hands to right hip and twist A's right arm.

B Then step over the right shoulder with left foot and lock A's right elbow (*Ude-hishigi*).

Kyuhonme (No. 9) Oshitaoshi from *Pin'an Godan*

(Oshitaoshi = push down)

A Step left foot, then right foot forward, right *Chudan Oi-zuki*.
B Move left foot to the left a little, then step right foot forward and make right *Moto-dachi* stance. At the same time, block A's punch with right *Chudan Sasae-uke*.

B Left *Ura-zuki* to the rib (*Inazuma*, right SP-16/SP-21).

B Step left foot forward and push both hands forward to twist A's right arm (*Udegarami*).

B Lower the body and push A down to the ground on his back. Drop right knee to his floating rib (*Getsuei*, LV-14).

196

B Insert left hand under A's right arm, then lift it and take hold of his right fist.

B Lift right arm and hold your own left hand with the right from the top.

B Lift and twist his right wrist.

B Keep twisting his right wrist with right hand and strike his temple (*Kasumi*, GB-5 and *Ryomo*, GB-3) with left *Shotei-uchi*.

Kyusho (vital points) used in these sets

Head

Jinchu	GV-26	between nose and mouth
Miken	–	between eyebrows
Sankon	–	just above the bridge of nose
Bikou	–	just below the bridge of nose
Ryomo	GB-3	lower temple
Kasumi	GB-5	upper temple

Neck

Keichu	GV-15	back of neck
(Shikon	ST-9	both sides of throat)
Kochu	–	just below the Adam's apple
Koka	ST-10	both sides of Adam's apple
Hichu	CV-22	small hole just above the sternum
Matsukaze	LI-17	right front side of neck
Murasame	LI-17	left front side of neck
Erishita	ST-12	just behind the centre of each collar bone

Front of trunk

Inazuma	SP-16	right rib
Denko	/SP-21	left rib
Getsuei	LV-14	floating rib
Suigetsu	CV-14	solar plexus
Myoken	SP-14	sides of lower abdomen

Back

Sakkatsu	GV-11	between shoulder blades
Ushiro-Denko	BL-44	left side of hind floating rib
Ushiro-Inazuma		right side of hind floating rib
Ushiro-Getsuei	GB-25	kidney
(Kame-no-o	GV-1	tail bone)

Arm

Soto-Hijizume	TH-10	outer side of elbow
Uchi-Hijizume	HC-3	inner side of elbow

Leg

Kekkai	SP-10	inside upper knee
Shikkoku	BL-54	back of knee

Glossary

of terms used in this volume

age-uke	rising block	mae-geri	front kick
chudan	mid-level	maeken-zuki	leading hand punch
chudan-zuki	punch to the mid-level	ma-hanmi	side-facing body position
empi	elbow (or, elbow strike)	mawashi hiji-ate	roundhouse elbow strike
fumikae	change step	migi	right
gedan	lower level	morote-uke	double arm block
gyaku-hanmi	reverse quarter facing body position	moto-dachi	base stance
		musubi-dachi	heel together, toes open, stance
gyaku-waza	joint attacking (twisting and over-stretching) techniques	nagashi-uke	let-go block
gyaku-zuki	reverse punch	naotte	'at attention' position
haishu-uke	back of hand block	nekoashi-dachi	cat stance
hanmi	quarter facing body position	ninoude-uke	forearm block
harai-uke	sweeping block	niren-zuki	double punch (two consecutive punches)
heiko-dachi	parallel stance		
heisoku-dachi	feet together stance	nukite	spear hand
hidari	left	oi-zuki	step forward and punch with the arm which is same side as the stepping foot
hiji-ate	elbow strike		
hiki hazushi	pull and disengage		
hikite	pull-back hand	rei	bow
hiza-geri	knee kick	riai	principles and theories
hokei	pair work to practise principles	ryo-uke	two arm block
		sasae-uke	supported block
ippon-seoi-nage	one arm over the shoulder throw	shiko-dachi	square stance (Sumo stance)
		shizen-dachi heiko	parallel natural stance
irimi	'enter body' foot and body work	shomen	square facing body position
		shotei harai-uke	sweeping block using palm heel
jodan	upper level		
kagi-zuki	hook punch	shotei osae-uke	press-down block using palm heel
kaisho kosa-uke	open hand crossed arms block		
		shuto	knife hand (hand sword)
kamae	guarding position	shuto-barai	sweeping block with Shuto
kentsui	hammer-fist	shuto-uchi	knife hand strike
kentsui-uchi	hammer-fist strike	shuto-uke	knife hand block
kiai	shout (with spirit)	sokkutsu-dachi	side bent stance
kiri keashi	quick turning and turning back of the body	solar plexus	the upper front part of the abdomen just below the rib cage; nerves at the pit of the stomach
kokutsu-dachi	back stance (rear bent stance)		
		soto-hachiji-dachi	toes point out stance (outward letter eight stance)
kosa-dachi	crossed stance		
kosa-uke	crossed arms block		
maeashi-geri	kick using front leg	sukui-uke	scooping block

..ni	body drop throw	ushiro	back (rear)
..ken-zuki	vertical fist punch	ushiro-zuki	punch towards back
..ate-nukite	vertical spear hand	yoi	'ready' position
tenshin	'change direction' foot and body work	yoko-barai	side sweeping block
		yoko-geri	side kick
tsugi-ashi	follow step	yoko-uke	side block
tsuki	punch (thrust)	yoriashi	slide in
uchi-otoshi	'strike down' block	zanshin	reserved mind
ura-uchi	back fist strike	zenkutsu-dachi	long stance (forward bent stance)
ura-zuki	reversed fist punch		

RESOURCES

Videos are available by Keiji Tomiyama which include these katas and practice sets plus a number of other fundamental and advanced katas and other subjects.

All information about these and other training aids, seminars worldwide and/or details about membership of the Shito-ryu Karate-do Kofukan International organization can be obtained by e-mailing to the following address:

secretary@kofukan.com

or visit our web site at **http://www.kofukan.com**